HELL WITH THE FIRE OUT

Hell
with the
Fire Out

*A History
of the Modoc War*

ARTHUR QUINN

ff

Faber and Faber, Inc.
Boston   London

Copyright © 1997 by Arthur Quinn

Library of Congress Cataloging-in-Publication Data

Quinn, Arthur.
    Hell with the fire out : a history of the Modoc War / Arthur Quinn.
        p.   cm.
    ISBN 0-571-19903-8
    1. Modoc Indians—Wars, 1873.   I. Title.
E83.87.Q56   1997
973'.049741—dc20   96-43421
                                                                CIP

Jacket design © Adrian Morgan at Red Letter Design
Printed in the United States of America

The winning of battles is not determined between men who plan and deliberate, who make a resolution and carry it out, but between men who are drained of these faculties, transformed, fallen either to the level of inert matter, which is all passivity, or to the level of blind forces, which are all momentum. This is the final secret of war.

—SIMONE WEIL

The strong do what they will, the weak what they must.

—THUCYDIDES

Preface

Shortly after I finished writing this book, I began to live it.

The book is about human passivity, how sometimes, especially in war, human beings seem but the playthings of the demonic. Then human willing, even of the good, becomes a delusory act. The weak frequently recognize this, the strong but rarely.

Of course, none of us is in the last analysis strong. We will all suffer, and know we will suffer, death. Reprieves, if they come, are temporary. Death is always there before us, as an inevitable coming attraction.

There is much death in the narrative that follows, but I hope I show it mostly in its ordinariness, its routineness, and only occasionally in its heroic dress. Death be not proud, human beings neither.

The death of an individual, like the rising and setting of the sun, like the changing of the winds, like the blowing of dust from here to there and back again, is scarcely worth mentioning. The rising and falling of nations, also.

The narrative that follows, therefore, is stark, in intention as stark as the Lava Beds that are its main setting. The events are hellish, without even the drama of a punishing fire. Hell with the fire out.

Over Christmastide 1995, almost half a world from home, I began to suffer an odd clumsiness on my left side. Then, in less than a week, I was entirely helpless. A brain tumor was diagnosed, of a type normally—some said, always—fatal. Two major operations ensued, successful within their limits. And I became for most of a year a patient, someone routinely dependent upon the kindness and competence of others for the most basic things, including mere survival.

My chief surgeon gives to all his patients a little card with sentences of advice, all very sensible and based on decades of experience. I am sure that card has done immense good. But none for me. It reminded me of the kind of list my wife, in exasperation, would make for me when, absentminded as I am, I went out for errands by myself.

"Get a half gallon of low fat milk. Also a loaf of sandwich bread. Don't forget the dry cleaning. And make sure to come to terms with your own mortality."

The drugs were a harrowing education in themselves. Steroids allowed me to experience homocidal rages and bottomless depressions. "Anyone in your condition who is not depressed," a sensible psychiatrist consoled, "ought to have his head examined." I had not wept since my father died, more than a decade before. Now I wept daily, sometimes hourly.

Antidepressants did no good, except to make me a falling-down drunk. However, drunks don't fall just in one direction (unless there is a wind), whereas I on antidepressants had an undeniable penchant for suddenly pitching forward. Exciting if you happen to be walking downhill, as I was the first time it hit me.

Anticonvulsives, on the other hand, made my thoughts move through my mind as if through molasses, leaving behind a trail of confusion and forgetfulness. There were times I could have passed the entrance exam for "nursing home resident with tenure." To play five-card draw with my poker buddies was a problem in differential equations. And they will probably never forgive me that one night, thanks to a run of extraordinary cards, the moron won significant money off them. (I'm still winning, months later, but not because of luck.)

"We have to keep you away from the FDA," a nurse said. "If they used you as a test subject, we'd never get any new drugs."

Mixed in with the constant fear, there were also episodes of the bizarre and the weird. For a short time I had the nose of a dog. I could smell what someone was eating three rooms away, and made myself less than popular at home by suggesting to family members that they use mouthwash and deodorant more frequently. At my birthday dinner in September I effortlessly identified the Napa Valley region where the delicious chardonnay came from. "This flintiness is characteristic of the wines from Carneros, the effect of the gravelly soil." I had heard other people say such things, but had not myself except in guess or bluff. Now I was sure without checking the label.

Other entertainments. Off and on for about a month, I had three hands, two left, one right. Don't even ask me how I figured that out, it took two days.

Drugs I had been off for months would occasionally reappear, uninvited, for a brief visit. One morning, after a bad night, I woke up ready to kill some neighbors who left their front light on. I ranted and ranted until I began to use obscenities that had not passed my lips in anger since adolescence. Then I suddenly realized this was not me speaking but my old friend Steroid.

I knew double vision when I saw it, thanks to a beaning in Little League. But I had not realized, until after my operations, that it could be so doubled you would not be able to stand. For a brief while standing required self-imposed blindness. But I worked out a compromise of sorts in order to get around. Shuffle a few paces, then peek.

At one point, in the hospital, while I was still partly under anaesthetic, I had what could only be described as the beginning of an angelic visitation. But I immediately shooed the angel away, having already decided I was going to find nothing good in my suffering.

I hated what was happening to me. I would not let it become my road to Damascus. When a clergyman friend visited not long after the angel, all the piety I could muster was, "Jesus! I hope this is not the last rites."

I do hope I did not actually say that, but the memory is distinct. Perhaps I just thought it. Of course, even if I said it, I could always contend that the exclamation point was really a comma, and I was praying, not cursing. Did I mention I was educated by the Jesuits?

My illness did have one lasting effect on this book. I had intended, once I finished a decent draft, to walk the Lava Beds, to check my descriptions. My illness made that impossible.

The more I think about that, the less I regret it. The Lava Beds are a cursed place. You will not convince me otherwise.

So I will never return there, willingly.

Of the many generosities that allowed me to finish this book, two examples must stand for the rest. A friend of more than thirty years flew across the continent when he instinctively realized that I was daunted by the task of final revisions. Thank you, Tom Mathews.

David and Anne Ramsay, throughout the ordeal, were my medical guides, advocates, and occasional chastisers, occasional chastisement being essential with someone who is, by personal inclination and metaphysical conviction, decidedly noncompliant. They and my family kept me on a path to possible recovery—a path, more often than not, I could not see, would not believe others saw. Words cannot express. . . .

That I am still alive today and able to contemplate new writing projects is due to the extraordinary treatment I received at the University of California at San Francisco, much of that treatment relying on techniques only recently available. At a time when the level of government funding for medical research seems at risk, those of us who have benefitted must speak up.

Also, after twenty-five years of being bounced from press to press, I now seem to have found a home, thanks to the efforts of my agent, Thomas D'Evelyn, and the good taste of Faber editors, such as Valerie Cimino.

Finally: In writing my narrative I have made two hard decisions with which some readers might strongly and reasonably disagree. First, those on one side of this conflict I have frequently called "Americans." By this I mean, of course, "citizens of the United States of America." To call them "whites," as some sympathetic readers have suggested to me, is to emphasize that this was a war between races. I prefer rather to view it as fundamentally a war between nations, one very large, the other very small. So most Modocs viewed it, as near as I can tell. So eventually did the United States government view it. There were those who took the racial view. They were the worst elements on both sides. Or so it seems to me.

Second, the surviving sources, while providing ample accounts of many events, are maddeningly sketchy with verbal exchanges. Usually, for instance, we do not even know for certain in what language a negotiation was conducted: English, Modoc, or Chinook (a trading language of the region).

I decided to accept as accurate any recorded conversation that is neither inherently implausible nor contradicted by better sources. Anyone who regards this handling of the record as irresponsible for a historian should simply read and judge what follows as historical fiction, with my blessing.

HELL WITH THE FIRE OUT

1

MEACHAM AND HIS PARTY were approaching the *wikiup* of Captain Jack when the guard sitting on the roof shouted, "One man come! No more!"

Alone, Meacham started up the rise to the entrance of the Modoc *wikiup*. From the outside, the lodge looked like a huge oblong basket turned face-down on a mound of earth, a small fort, perfect for a people so warlike they were always ready for an attack.

Meacham had counted thirteen lodges in this village, all normal lodges about twenty to thirty feet long and twelve feet wide. To enter them, white man and Indian alike had to scramble up the steps dug into the steep slope of their earthen coverings.

Meacham had been on his way up the steps to Captain Jack's *wikiup* when the guard had shouted the order. He knew that when he reached the opening he would then have to descend a ladder of rawhide ropes. Under ordinary circumstances he might first have turned to order the rest of his party to do as the guard told them. However, when he reached the entrance, he could just make out the faces of the warriors within. They were painted for war. He knew then that he might not reach the bottom of that ladder alive.

Alfred Benjamin Meacham—or rather A. B. Meacham, as he usually signed himself—was the head federal Indian agent for Oregon. He had come to the northern borderlands of California this morning of December 22, 1869, to try to convince a band of Modocs to return to the reservation they shared uncomfortably with the Klamaths. His mission was in keeping with the federal policy of consolidating the Western tribes in order to open more land for settlers. Most of the Modocs, under the headman Old Schonchin, were living on the reservation peacefully. But

3

this band of Modocs, led by an aspiring headman little more than thirty years old, did not want to live with the Klamaths, especially because the reservation was on Klamath land.

There had been a time, according to their own traditions, when the Klamaths and Modocs had been a single people, but the Modocs had seceded and moved south. "Modoc," according to one account, simply meant "southern people" in the Klamath tongue.

For generations after the split, the Klamaths and the Modocs had been enemies, or at least rivals. Their *wikiups* and much of the rest of their material culture might have been indistinguishable to American eyes, but these two peoples developed quite different reputations among the settlers who were starting to fill the border country of California and Oregon.

The Klamaths had found it easy to adapt to white ways. Their land was fertile, and they could produce many items to trade with the settlers for horses and other things they coveted. The Modocs, in contrast, had moved to badlands after the split. The price of their independence was a new home in an area dominated by lava beds.

The few lakes there, tule jungles teeming with wildlife, did provide plentiful food, fuel, and the raw materials of their daily life and economy. The staple of the Modoc diet was the tubers of the ipos plant, supplemented in the spring by the soft and milky bulbs of the camus and the juicy fresh roots of the desert parsley—for variety they could gather water lily seeds, pine nuts, and various berries, including the wild strawberry. The Modocs were skilled fishermen, and the two runs of suckers in their streams were truly prodigious. The run in March produced individual fish of ten to fifteen pounds, in numbers many more than the Modocs could use. Trout were plentiful in the summer and winter, although then the Modocs had to compete with the large population of wintering bald eagles. The land also yielded deer, antelope, and groundhogs as well as the occasional elk, mountain sheep, and bear, although the bear was dangerous to take. Most of the root and fish harvest was dried for the winter.

The Modoc land abundantly satisfied their traditional needs, despite its forbidding landscape. So they gave it a name that roughly translated as "Smiles of God." But this god did not smile on trade with the whites, for the region provided nothing whites considered valuable enough to trade for horses, cloth, and the other manufactured items the Modocs soon came to regard as necessities. Instead, the Modocs stole them from settlers, murdering those who got in the way—or so the more hot-headed Americans claimed. And Meacham knew there was some truth to this claim.

A southern branch of the Oregon Trail ran through Modoc country. It had been established by father and uncle, Lindsay and Jesse Applegate, now in their early old age. Jesse and Lindsay were without question the most influential Americans in southern Oregon. Almost every activity of any consequence to southern Oregon these days now had one Applegate or another connected to it, usually Lindsay's sons Ivan and Oliver. Ivan Applegate, who worked in the reservation system, was in Meacham's party that December morning.

After the Applegate Trail opened in 1846, the Modocs had grown skilled at sneak attacks on unsuspecting wagon trains. Their great war chief, Schonchin, had led them. Now nearly a quarter century had passed. Schonchin was called Old Schonchin; a kindly old man, he had adjusted well to reservation life back at Klamath, but his legacy of war lived on.

At the center of Modoc territory, one spot on the shore of Tule Lake was now known as Bloody Point. It was an obvious place for a tired wagon train to camp, but the high tule grass provided perfect cover for approaching warriors—and, once they broke through the defenses, there was no escape. They killed the white men, rode off with the horses, and treated the surviving women and children as slaves or prostitutes.

Meacham knew that the Modocs, and for that matter the Klamaths, saw nothing wrong with prostitution, or what seemed like prostitution to American eyes. Their willingness to sell their women, even family members, made the Modocs popular in Yreka, the wild mining town that was booming only a day's ride from their territory. The prospectors of Yreka, who welcomed the Modocs, and the settlers of southern Oregon, who feared them, detested each other in the bargain, the Modocs serving as their bond of hate.

Meacham was an odd man to be faced with all this. He was tall, portly, and balding. He had a full dark beard like Ulysses S. Grant's and looked older than his forty-three years. He was careful about his appearance, always dressing formally in suit and tie, the sign of a man singularly out of place in the Far West. He was a Methodist, a "strict temperance man" who believed the strong should forgo drink for the sake of the weak who cannot control their thirst. In another time and place, A. B. Meacham would have been a vegetarian and a pacifist. The cruelty of frontier life disgusted him.

As a boy Meacham had seen the Sacs and Foxes removed from their beautiful valley in Iowa after the Black Hawk War. The morning of their departure was still fresh in his memory thirty years later—"photographed on my mind," he wrote.

The Indians had gone peaceably that day, with no bloodshed, no violence. Their leaders had struck the best deal they could. Their eviction, he wrote, was accomplished "under the sanction of law, and in the shade of Church-steeples, and with the sanctimonious semblance of honesty and justice." Even then, as a boy, he recognized "the advantage which the powerful always have over the weak."

The powerful may always have this advantage, but Meacham believed they should not use it. He became an early and uncompromising abolitionist. His strong support for Grant and the Republican party in the presidential election of 1870 had led to his appointment as Indian agent for Oregon. He had sought this appointment earlier, but was denied it because he had opposed Andrew Johnson's harsh treatment of the defeated South.

Meacham was typical of those Republicans who urged President Grant to adopt a peaceable or "Quaker" policy toward the western Indians. To his contemporaries, his aversion to cruelty, an aversion to the strong taking advantage of the weak, must have made him seem at times a little mad.

Despite the many Indian customs he admired, he could not reconcile himself to the roasting of live crickets. "Think, for a moment," he reflected, "of the helpless, writhing mass of animated nature in a hot furnace—a great black heap of insects being stirred with poles until they are roasted, while their inhuman torturers are apparently unconscious of the fact that these crickets are complete organisms, each with a separate existence, struggling for life." But he saw the indifference of the Indians to the writhing crickets as typical of human nature. The cricket roast reminded Meacham of an American clambake: "How little human sympathy goes out for helpless things."

As Meacham approached the Modoc village earlier that morning, he had to cross Lost River, the stream that connected Tule Lake with Klamath Lake, the chief lake of the Modoc territory with the chief lake of the Klamath territory. Lost River flowed underground part way, lost to sight, much as the historical connection between these two tribes had been lost in the past, a connection Meacham now meant to retrieve.

To cross Lost River, Meacham and his party had to use Natural Bridge, a twenty-foot-wide ledge of rocks submerged a few feet under the water that made the river fordable. If you did not look carefully, you did not see Natural Bridge at all. All you saw was a trail leading up on one side and away on another. Wasn't that what peacemakers always sought—natural but invisible bridges across the unpredictable currents of human affairs?

A. B. Meacham was no longer in a moralizing mood when he climbed down the ladder into Captain Jack's *wikiup*. Before turning his back to use the ladder, he had seen through the flickering light grim faces in traditional warpaint—streaks of white clay and circles of red ochre. This glance, he later wrote, filled his mind with a single, simple feeling: *I should be somewhere else—anywhere else.* As he clumsily worked himself down the rawhide ladder, he found himself wondering how it would feel to take a bullet or an arrow in the back.

Finally down, he turned to face the Modocs, perhaps fifty of them crowded into Captain Jack's smoky *wikiup.* Jack was the leader of this breakaway band, but also an advocate of peace between the Modocs and the Americans, like Meacham himself. When their eyes met this day, Jack just stared at Meacham, refusing to speak, refusing to shake hands, refusing even his offer of a smoke.

Meacham did his best to look confident. He slowly filled his own pipe, lit it and puffed a few times, hoping that his hand was not noticeably trembling. Suddenly he felt a terrible loneliness, although just a shout away his friends and colleagues were ready to rush the lodge.

Within the *wikiup*, crowded, tense, Meacham tried to keep himself calm by surveying the Modocs before him, trying to connect names and faces. All these Modocs had been given American nicknames by the prospectors of Yreka. The Modocs had accepted them without complaint, as they had accepted many American customs. They generally cut their hair short, American-style, wore the clothes of the cowboy, and had mastered many of the cowboy's skills.

Captain Jack himself was easy to identify because of the deference the others showed him. Short—almost squat—but powerfully built, he was handsome, with strong chiseled features and skin that had a bronze tinge. Meacham also picked out Jack's two brothers. Black Jim had skin as black as a crow's wing, a character as reliable as a snake's. Jack's other brother, Humpy Joe, with the hunch on his back, was tolerated by the rest, but not a factor in council.

At Jack's right hand was Scarfaced Charley, a Modoc much respected by the whites who knew him. A huge V-shaped scar marred his left cheek. He had tried to hitch a ride on a stage in Yreka, but had fallen off, almost leaving his cheek behind. As a boy he had seen his father killed for nothing by a white man. About six feet tall, reputedly a great warrior, he was someone on whose word you could stake your life.

Schonchin John, a formidable and treacherous enemy, was recognizable by the flecks of white in his hair. Brother of Old Schonchin, the headman of the reservation Modocs, he was Captain Jack's rival. Schonchin John intended to become headman of this band by opposing Jack's policy of peace toward settlers. In appearance Schonchin John, more than any of the others, fit the white stereotype of a "savage."

Hooker Jim could have been John's son, or even grandson. To Meacham he looked much younger than his twenty-two years and seemed out of place in this council—a boy among men. But he was the Modocs' best tracker and marksman, not someone to whom you would show your back.

Finally, there was Curley Headed Doctor, the shaman of the band and the most malevolent of the Modocs. He used all his medicine against Captain Jack's spirit of compromise. If Schonchin John fit the white stereotype, Curley Headed Doctor was the white scourge, a master of the witchcraft of racial hate.

Meacham studied the faces in the uneven light of the fire, determined not to be the first to speak, hoping that the first Modoc to talk would be a friend of peace. Scarfaced Charley broke the silence. He spoke in the English patois the Modocs and Americans used when they had no interpreter. His deep bass voice was unusual for a Modoc.

"What you want? What for you come? Jack, he not send for you! He in his country! What for you come here? You not his *tyee*! He don't know you!"

Tyee was one Modoc word all settlers knew; it meant "headman" or "chief." Charley was denying Meacham's authority. "*Halluimetilicum!*" he shouted, breaking into Modoc. "Stranger" or "outsider" or "intruder"—it meant something like that. A stranger, Meacham most certainly felt himself to be. Charley then concluded his vehement speech in patois.

"Captain Jack want to see you, him come your home! He no want you come here! You go away! Let him 'lone! He no want talk you! You go home!"

Meacham did his best to assert his authority. He tried to speak in sentences as simple and plain as Charley's.

He *was* their new *tyee*, he said. He had been appointed by the President. They may not think of themselves as his friend, but he *was* their friend. He had come to see them and to listen to Captain Jack. He was not afraid to do that. He was a big *tyee*. He did not have to ask anyone's permission to listen or talk.

Meacham was gambling. His guess was that Jack was still on the side of peace but had to oppose the belligerents in his band. Meacham implied, delicately, that if Jack allowed others to dictate to whom he would speak and to whom he would listen, he was no *tyee* himself. Jack understood. He answered calmly.

"I have nothing to say you would like to hear. All your people are liars and swindlers. I do not believe half that is told me. I am not afraid to hear you talk."

To Meacham's taunt Jack had made his own riposte. Why be afraid to listen to someone you already know to be a liar? Still, he had given Meacham an opening. Now the agent asked that the rest of his party, the rest of the liars and swindlers, be permitted to join him in here. Jack agreed.

The order was given. One by one, Meacham's party clambered down the rope ladder. Most had almost as much difficulty as Meacham. Donald McKay, however, almost jumped down in his eagerness; and Tobey

Riddle came down holding her hide skirt tightly with a hand, just as dictated by Modoc modesty.

Tobey Riddle and her husband Frank, Meacham's interpreters, were living proof that whites and Modocs could rise above their common hatred. Seven years before, after a hard Kentucky childhood, Frank Riddle had been prospecting near Tule Lake when Modoacus, an uncle of Captain Jack, had approached his cabin and offered to sell him a twelve-year-old Modoc girl. Riddle hesitated for a time, but the girl and her father kept reappearing. Riddle finally admitted to himself that when he looked at this plump Indian girl with her unusual reddish brown hair he felt, as he put it in his half-literate way, "a goneness in my heart." So he bought her for two horses. They had lived together ever since. They had a small boy. They had named him Jefferson Davis Riddle.

Living with a bought Modoc woman looked like backsliding to slavery, at least from the strict abolitionist point of view. So after Meacham became Indian agent, he had pressured Riddle to send his squaw back to her people or to marry her. Riddle, despite his admiration for Jefferson Davis and the ways of the Old South, decided to act on the goneness in his heart. He married Tobey. They were now man and wife—a living example that relations between these two very different peoples could go the way of love—or hate.

Another of Meacham's party, the scout Don McKay, came down on the side of murder. Half-Indian, half-white, he made his living off Indian troubles. The Americans had learned that when they went to war with Indians, rival tribes took the opportunity to settle old scores by helping the Americans, often fighting side-by-side with them. McKay was just the person to organize and lead the Indian forces for the whites. He lived in perpetual eagerness for war, relishing its brutalities.

The negotiations finally began. Captain Jack firmly controlled the agenda. He brought out a collection of documents. He knew the Americans set great store by such pieces of paper, much as his own people revered their oral traditions. These documents included letters Captain Jack had preserved from prominent Americans of the region, especially Yrekans, attesting to his reliability. Captain Jack and his people were not liars or swindlers. You could believe all that they said.

After this prologue, Captain Jack waited patiently while Meacham and his party read all the papers, the Americans feigning interest in them. Meacham had heard how two judges in Yreka, who comprised the little law there was in that place, had supported the Modocs. Judge Elijah Steele, on his own initiative, had negotiated a treaty with the Modocs to give them legal title to their traditional land, an exercise in decency rejected by the federal government. The documents Jack presented had no legal authority. Still, Meacham and those with him looked at each with care.

By this time the day was already getting late. Dusk had fallen early because of the high ground to the west. Within the *wikiup* it was hard to see anything clearly. The light of the council fire cast an uneven, unwholesome radiance on the faces of the negotiators.

Meacham then suggested that the Americans be permitted to set up a camp nearby; talks would resume the next morning. Captain Jack agreed. He offered provisions to Meacham, though he did not think the Americans would care for them. The Modocs were now living on dried fish and roots. Captain Jack added mischievously that he had no flour, no coffee, no sugar, no whiskey—and as near as Captain Jack could tell white *tyees* could not survive without these. There is no word for what Meacham, the teetotaler, thought about the mention of whiskey. The Americans had brought their own supplies, Meacham assured Captain Jack, but had left them a short ride away. The wagons could be brought up tomorrow. In the meantime, Meacham was happy to accept Captain Jack's hospitality.

So Meacham's party did have an Indian dinner, but off by themselves. With a certain flourish, Captain Jack produced some fresh fish—probably trout—which the Americans roasted in sagebrush embers. The night was cold, with a wind off nearby Tule Lake. The sky was brilliant, crisply lit with stars. The sounds of animals rustling, cooing, and howling filled the night. The Americans caught glimpses of raccoons and coyotes at the edge of their camp, looking to snatch food. The Americans were all alert to any movement or sound, but they were not worrying about thieving animals.

They finally retired around their guttering campfire, each with his weapon within reach, Tobey cuddling up to Frank Riddle. They all settled down to sleep, or to pretend to sleep.

The next morning, they were up at first light. Once the supply wagons pulled into the camp, Meacham offered to reciprocate Modoc hospitality by treating them to a proper American breakfast: coffee with plenty of sugar, hard tack, beef, bacon. He noticed that all the Modocs waited until the Americans had begun to eat heartily before they ventured a taste. He knew why, and it had nothing to do with etiquette. He was seeing the legacy of Ben Wright.

In the 1850s no white man was more feared in the California border country, by Indian and white alike, than Ben Wright. The wagon train that had carried him west had come under Indian attack (not by Modocs), and a young girl he loved was killed. The disaster turned him to killing as a way of life. He enjoyed it, bragged about it, taking not just the scalps of his victims, but their noses, ears, fingers. He wallowed in his reputation. He let his hair grow long and dressed flamboyantly.

He soon directed his attention to the Modocs. When reports reached him that they were massacring wagon trains, he led punitive expeditions, though without much success. Finally, in 1852 he invited the Modocs, under a flag of truce, to peace negotiations on Tule Lake. He laid out a great feast for them, seasoning it liberally with strychnine. The Modocs noticed the white men were not eating, and held off— perhaps they had been warned—but it made no difference. Wright and his men pulled out concealed weapons and opened up. Of the forty-six Modocs at the peace conference only five survived; one of these was Schonchin John.

White settlers treated Wright as a hero. They gave him an Oregon Indian agency on the coast for his achievements. A few years later, in a drunken rage, he ripped the clothes off an Indian interpreter who had displeased him, and then drove her naked through the streets of a mining town with a whip. Not long afterwards she had him murdered. She personally ate his heart.

No one, either Modoc or American, seriously doubted the general truth of this story, although a few Americans questioned the part about poison, and more than a few thought that the Modocs had gotten only what was coming to them.

For the Modocs, the episode with Ben Wright proved that Americans could never be trusted, even under a flag of truce, even when proposing peace. Meacham certainly did not fault them for their caution. He did not believe, however, that Wright's heinous act should poison forever the trust between these two peoples. To his mind, Modocs and Americans ought to be able to live together in peace, despite murderous memories of Bloody Point and Ben Wright.

After breakfast was finished, the negotiations began again. Meacham was now hopeful—and his hope rested firmly on Captain Jack who had been, in Meacham's judgment, so admirably straightforward. The new council session had scarcely begun before Meacham realized that he had misjudged him.

Meacham opened the proceedings by narrating the history that had brought him here on this cold, bright December day in 1869. He produced the treaty of 1864 in which the Modocs agreed to move from the Lost River area to the reservation that had been prepared for them and the Klamaths and the small band of Paiute Snakes. Captain Jack did not seem pleased that Meacham had brought the actual treaty. But Meacham was determined to use it as the basis for negotiating the return of Captain Jack and his band.

Captain Jack quickly made it clear that he meant to concede nothing. He offered, in Meacham's words, the "careful, cautious kind of diplomacy that does not come to a point, but continually seeks to shirk responsibility." Americans were liars and swindlers, and Captain Jack wouldn't believe half of what they earnestly assured him. Meacham now understood that the Modoc's first sentence to him the day before was serious: "I have nothing to say that you will want to hear."

Captain Jack began by denying that he was bound by the 1864 treaty. He had neither participated in the negotiations nor signed the finished document. This was a lie. So Meacham patiently demonstrated to Captain Jack what they both knew to be true. He produced three witnesses from his own party—an American, a Klamath, and a Modoc—all of whom swore that Captain Jack had participated in the negotiations and had signed the treaty. He said he could show Captain Jack the very place on the treaty where he had made his mark. But why do that, since Captain Jack had accepted the goods that the government provided in confirmation of the treaty, perhaps as much as

$10,000 worth? Members of his band should be able to remember that he had distributed these goods to them.

Having lost his first line of defense, Captain Jack asked where on the reservation the government expected him to settle now. He seemed surprised when Meacham told him he could take any unoccupied land he wanted. Jack then specified a particular friend he wanted to live near, a Klamath named Link River Jack. Meacham assured him that this was fine.

Meacham now felt he had won the first skirmish with Captain Jack, but he knew better than to think that this meant the Modocs would return to the Klamath reservation. Captain Jack did not have the clearly defined power of the American officials. He was the leader of these Modocs, but he had to honor the consensus of the group. When he argued (as he did today against returning to the reservation), Meacham could not be certain whether he was advocating his own view or following the group's. If the latter (as Meacham suspected was the case), then rebutting his arguments only undercut his leadership. Scoring debating points did not mean that the band would change its mind. It might only strengthen Schonchin John.

What happened next did not surprise Meacham, but it worried him. The shaman, Curley Headed Doctor, rose. Here was the keeper of the Modoc traditions, and Curley Headed Doctor regarded them as the antithesis of reservation life.

Curley Headed Doctor would speak only in Modoc.

"*Mekigamblaketu,*" he said emphatically. "We won't go there."

Then he added, "*Otwekautuxe.*" Those who understood him braced themselves. The expression could mean "I am done talking." That was bad enough. But it could also mean "The time is now," exactly what a Modoc would say when he was giving the signal to attack.

Tobey and Frank Riddle immediately grew alert. Pleading with the Modocs, Tobey said, "The white *tyee* talks right. His heart is good, strong. Go with him now." Frank added his own exhortations. While they were arguing in Modoc, the scout McKay was saying to the Americans, "Be on your guard. Don't let them get the drop on us." Applegate glanced quickly about for an exit. No way out.

Captain Jack started to move away from the council. Now it was Meacham's turn to plead, and to threaten. He said, not quite truthfully, that Captain Jack had already promised to come to the reservation. The wagons were ready to take his old people and children. If he didn't come, this could be the end for his people.

For the first time Meacham shouted: "We came for you and we are not going back! You must come!"

This was too much like an order, and Captain Jack bristled, challenging Meacham to specify what he would do if the Modocs refused. Meacham responded that they would whip him until he changed his mind.

Captain Jack's response—and its chivalrous contempt—Meacham never forgot: "I would be ashamed to fight so few men with all mine."

Meacham replied that he had enough men to kill plenty of Modocs before they were all dead—and many others would come after.

At that moment, Captain Jack, openly disdainful, said two things Meacham would hear repeatedly from him over the next few years. He would never fire the first shot—and he was not afraid to die.

The council was over. The Modocs retired to Captain Jack's *wikiup*, the Americans to their camp. Withdrawing from the village was out of the question. If the Modocs chose, they could simply pick the Americans off along the route. If attacked in the village, the Americans would quickly be overwhelmed, but they could at least make a stand. Captain Jack had promised that he would not fire the first shot. But another Modoc, following Curley Headed Doctor, might be more than happy to cut loose, and then Captain Jack would have to join in.

The Americans decided to send out a messenger to get military support. They told the Modocs their man was simply rounding up supply horses that had wandered off. In fact, he was to ride hard to Linkville, the closest town in Oregon, some twenty-five miles away and a center of anti-Modoc agitation, then lead enough soldiers back to the village to be within the sound of gunshot but out of sight. If the reinforcements heard gunshots at any point, they were to charge the village. Otherwise, they were to approach in orderly fashion the next morning, as if just happening by.

While the Americans were sitting around in the deepening night, once again chilled by a breeze off Tule Lake and now checking their weapons, the Modocs were holding their own private council in Captain Jack's *wikiup*. The Americans could hear a droning, sing-song chant.

Curley Headed Doctor was making medicine while the Modoc debated what to do with the intruders. Big medicine. If it worked, it would leave them all quite dead.

The council went on and on. The supporters of Curley Headed Doctor insisted on killing the Americans, while Captain Jack counseled peace. Then about midnight, with Captain Jack in the middle of a speech, a commotion broke out beyond the village. The dozing Americans were suddenly startled awake.

Horse hooves on hard ground. Breaking sagebrush. The rattling of sabers, the shouts of men. It was a cavalry charge.

The Linkville squad had taken along plenty of whiskey to protect the riders against the cold. By the time they drew near to the village they had consumed so much they could no longer remember the finer distinctions in their orders. They did remember that under certain circumstances they were to charge. So, just to be safe, they did charge. They were greeted by the Americans with surprise, relief, and mirth. Only Meacham seemed annoyed at the advancing drunks.

The Modocs, on the other hand, thought that they were about to be massacred. The white man *was* a liar and swindler, especially when offering peace. Ben Wright all over again.

As the cavalry charged, an extraordinary scramble occurred within the village, but the Modocs had been taken too much by surprise to offer resistance. Not a shot was fired, and the whiskey-fueled cavalry soon encircled all the Modocs in sight. Once the surrounded Modocs realized that they were not to be killed, they became docile. The Americans, weapons at the ready, threw a picket line around the Indians. Then everyone simply waited uneasily until dawn to sort out what had happened and what was to be done next.

At first light about a hundred Modocs were ordered to line up in single file. Of the band's fifty warriors, only a few had managed to slip away in the first moments of confusion, but these included Captain Jack and Curley Headed Doctor. The discovery disappointed the whites, who now had to disarm the remaining warriors.

At first the Modocs refused to give up their weapons. Then they saw that resistance was useless, and laid them down. All the while, a few women and old men were loudly professing loyalty to the Americans and thanking them for what had happened. Meacham chose to believe they were sincere, although they were simply trying to avoid bloodshed by calming everyone down, Modoc and American alike. The Americans then did their own part to soothe the Indians by issuing provisions. The Modocs were told that they were to be escorted back to the reservation soon, so they should pack up.

The problem remained of how to get Captain Jack and the others back to rejoin the band and accompany them. For the first time Meacham had to deal with Queen Mary, Captain Jack's sister. All the Americans had heard of her. She had her brother's strongly chiseled features, the same dignity of bearing. Even Americans who professed to be repelled by the appearance of Indian women admitted that she was extraordinarily beautiful.

And she knew it. Queen Mary had brought considerable wealth to her family. She had lived with a series of American prospectors in Yreka, perhaps as many as seven. She would agree to live with one, then clean him out. When he went back to prospecting, she would move on to the next. Everyone knew her pattern, yet there was always another man eager to have her.

Now she was speaking to the Americans on behalf of her brother. She boldly praised his escape. This was not cowardice on his part, she insisted, but good sense. Captain Jack was quite understandably wary, given past American treachery. But she was willing to try to find him and talk him into coming back. So while the Modocs were breaking up camp, Mary was sent off with an American guide to find her brother. She hardly needed help, but under the circumstances it was better to call the escort a guide than a guard.

The Modocs took a full day to get ready to leave. Those who had ponies rode them. Most of the others got into the American wagons. The rest walked. By the time the group had made its slow progress to Link River that night Mary had found Captain Jack. She sent a message that he and the others were prepared to negotiate their return.

Meacham was pleased and exasperated. As he admitted in his memoirs, he expected Captain Jack to act like one of Fenimore Cooper's noble savages, and he found it unseemly that the Modoc was so given to haggling. Haggling of any kind rubbed Meacham the wrong way. But he ordered his men and the Modocs to set up camp on

the Link River where they could stay until they could talk Captain
Jack back into the fold.

While they waited, Meacham's delicacy almost precipitated a new
crisis. He learned that an old Modoc woman had been left behind at the
Lost River camp. There was no point in bringing her along, the Modocs
said, since she was already too weak to work. But how would she survive? The Indians had left her with a little food and water and wood,
enough for her to die easily.

Meacham ordered the best stores he had—bread, sugar, meat, new
blankets—sent to her immediately. Once she was strong enough, she
was to be brought back and reunited with her loving family, though
Meacham could not identify the relatives. He loudly asked for a volunteer from the Modocs to carry out this errand of mercy—but none came
forward. No one wanted to interfere with the decision of another family, a decision in keeping with traditional practices. Finally a young
man stepped forward. But Meacham's relief almost immediately
turned to disgust when this good Samaritan quickly set a condition. If
the old woman happened to be dead or if she died on the way back, the
blankets and pony Meacham was supplying would be his. The agent
had no doubt that if the Modoc did not find the old woman dead he fully
intended to kill her.

Meacham now fell into what was for him a fury—a moral indigna-
tion deeply tinged with melancholy. Life was cruel enough. Why did
these people make it worse? And why did they pretend that they had
no moral obligations? He was determined to find out exactly who the
family was.

The inquiry was not easy, but finally he confronted the relatives, a
man and a woman. When he demanded they retrieve the old woman,
they suggested in turn that they be paid for their effort, and in advance. Meacham now thundered that they would go and they would not
be paid—and if anything happened to the old woman, it would be on
their heads. He, A. B. Meacham, their *tyee* appointed by Washington,
would personally see to it that they were fully punished.

So off they went grumpily. Eventually they returned with the old
woman, still alive but so weak she could not sit up on the pony without
the support of the woman—her daughter, as it turned out—who was
sitting behind her.

Meanwhile the negotiations with Captain Jack dragged out over several days. The bloodless defeat at the Lost River camp had undermined his authority. He did not want to be an object of ridicule for having run away—and certainly the Klamaths would ridicule him if they found out about this. He had a proposal. He did not want his warriors to come onto the reservation under guard. It was bad enough that they had been disarmed. The soldiers should be sent ahead to the fort near the Klamath reservation. Captain Jack and his men would then arrive only with the peace party headed by Meacham.

Meacham thought the demands "strange," but he continued to believe that the Modoc was acting in good faith, if a bit childishly, so he agreed.

The military squad was sent ahead to Fort Klamath, a relatively new fort, established in 1863 after the Applegates convinced the federal government to protect their vulnerable southern route against the Indians. Politics did its work, and the fort was established well away from Modoc country—or, as an outraged Lindsay Applegate said, "in a place where it entirely fails to accomplish the objects for which a post was ordered."

With the military squad safely on its way, the Modocs and Meacham's party left the Link River encampment on December 27, an extremely cold day. As they traveled over the mountain road between Link River and Klamath Lake, it got even colder. Meacham estimated the snow at twenty inches. Finally, on December 28, they arrived at the Klamath reservation.

The next day, while the Modocs were setting up their camp, Captain Jack insisted that Meacham prohibit any gambling—which he did, to the protests of the Klamaths. Both peoples enjoyed traditional gambling games, at times for very high stakes.

These games all involved marked pieces that one player arranged and kept hidden while the opponent tried to guess the arrangement by asking questions that the other player had to answer truthfully. The skillful gambler had to be able to read his opponent's mind, much like a good poker player (the game to which the Americans were addicted). Such games could leave bad blood between the losers and winners, especially since the winners augmented their pleasure by taunting the losers.

This was the last thing Captain Jack needed right before a peace negotiation with the Klamaths. Once gambling had started, Klamath and Modoc would be eager to wager against one another, and the whole peace settlement would be put at risk.

The Modoc camp was scattered over Modoc Point jutting out into Klamath Lake, with no obvious order except that each *wikiup* had easy access to water. There were some tents, but mostly traditional buildings, quickly framed with willow poles and covered with matting, blankets, or whatever else was handy. Most of the horses were put out to pasture in nearby meadows, nibbling the winter grass. Others were tied up near the lodges, at hand for immediate use.

On the second day after their arrival, the Modocs and the Klamaths began what they believed was their formal negotiation with Meacham. But the agent had already decided it was not to be a negotiation but a peace ceremony, a reaffirmation of the treaty of 1864 that had united the two tribes on the reservation.

Meacham selected an appropriate site at the foot of a mountain, under a great ponderosa pine. The Klamath arrived first, standing single file in a long line, with their able young chief David Allen at its head. The Modoc then came up, led by Captain Jack. Meacham did not like their demeanor; the Modoc looked to him reluctant and half-afraid. Captain Jack himself, however, was up to the situation. He positioned himself right across from David Allen, just a few feet away. There he could negotiate with David Allen, or, if a fight broke out, he would be the first to get at the Klamath chief. Meacham had ordered all the men to come unarmed. As near as he could tell, they had obeyed the order, but he couldn't be sure. He decided nonetheless to open the proceedings.

"You meet today in peace, to bury all the bad past, to make friends," he said. "You are of the same blood, of the same heart. You are to live as neighbors. This country belongs to you, all alike. Your interests are one. You can shake hands and be friends."

With these few words, Meacham mixed together the true and the doubtful. Modocs might concede that they were of the same blood as the Klamath, but they didn't believe they were of the same heart. That is why they had broken away, why they had fought the Modocs so often. That bloody past was not bad, at least when the Modocs were strong.

The Klamaths for their part knew perfectly well that this was their country, not Modoc country. Modoc country was two days away. The Modocs were guests on Klamath land, guests imposed by the Americans. They could perhaps be friends with their old rivals, but only if the Modocs behaved like guests, which they did not seem inclined to do.

Ignoring these realities, Meacham finished his little speech and began a carefully planned ritual. He placed a hatchet in the open space between Captain Jack and David Allen, amidst some loose pine boughs. He then handed each chief a pine bough. Simultaneously the two moved forward—and covered the hatchet with the boughs and stepped on the covering. Now, for the first time, they looked in each other's eyes. It was little more than a glance. Meacham found it inscrutable. Then they shook hands. To Meacham's pleasure, the shaking of hands was long and firm.

The ceremony was repeated by pair after pair of Modocs and Klamaths. They stepped forward from lines as carefully arranged as any receiving line in a lavish European court. The ritual took time, but it was essential. Every man had to show he agreed to bury the hatchet so all could be held accountable for any breech. Then David Allen began to speak. Standing rigidly erect, he looked directly at Captain Jack. As if for the first time, Meacham noticed that the Klamath was fully six feet tall. David Allen towered over Captain Jack.

"I see you. I see your eyes," he said. "Your skin is red like my own. I will show you my heart. We have long been enemies. Many of our brave people are dead. The ground is black with their blood. Their bones have been carried by the coyotes to the mountains, and scattered among the rocks. Our people are melting away like snow. We see the white chief is strong. The law is strong. We cannot be Indians longer. We must take the white man's law. The law our fathers had is dead. The white chief brought you here. We have made friends. We have washed each other's hands. They are not bloody now. We are friends. We have buried all the bad blood. We will not dig it up again. The white man sees us. God is looking at our hearts. The sun is a witness between us, the mountains are looking on us."

For a moment it seemed that David Allen had finished, but then he turned and gestured to the great pine tree—and for the first time something like emotion could be heard in his voice.

"This pine tree is a witness, O my people! When you see this tree, remember it is a witness that here we made friends with the Modocs. Never cut down that tree. Let the arm be broken that would hurt it. Let the hand die that would break a twig from it. So long as snow shall fall on Yainax Mountain, let it stand. So long as the white rabbit shall live in the groves, let it stand. Let our children play around it. Let the young people dance under its leaves, and let the old men smoke together in its shade. Let this tree stand forever, as a witness."

Then David Allen said plainly, "I have done."

All eyes turned to Captain Jack, and he began to speak, returning David Allen's fixed gaze.

It was immediately clear that the Modoc could not match the Klamath chief as a great orator. His voice was low and oddly modulated—"musical," Meacham thought. While Allen's words had come out chiseled in their distinctness, there was something hesitant, almost suppressed in Captain Jack's diction, as if he were groping to find the right words and not quite succeeding. What in Allen's mouth sounded dignified, even sublime, in Captain Jack's sounded vulnerable. The Modoc's words themselves expressed a lack of certainty. Coming from a noble savage, this made Meacham uneasy.

"The white chief brought me here. I feel ashamed of my people because they are poor. I feel like a man in a strange country without a father. My heart was afraid. I have heard your words. They warm my heart. I am not strange now. The blood is all washed from our hands. We are enemies no longer. We have buried the past. We have forgotten that we were enemies. We will not throw away the white chief's words. We will not hide them in the grass. I have planted a strong stake in the ground. I have tied myself with a strong rope. I will not dig up the stake. I will not break the rope. My heart is the heart of my people. I am their words. I am not speaking for myself. I speak their hearts. My heart comes up to the mouth. I cannot keep it down with a sharp stick. I am done."

David Allen had spoken as if he were the mouth and the heart of his people. At times he almost seemed to be speaking for the tree, the mountain and the sky. Captain Jack seemed to be speaking just for himself, never more so than when he claimed to be the words and heart of his people. Immediately after that, he admitted he was so overcome by emotion he could not go on. He stopped abruptly, without a true conclusion.

If the peace ceremony was also to some small degree a battle of eloquence, then the Klamaths had won a mighty victory against their old rivals. Captain Jack's premature conclusion could be heard as an unseemly surrender to David Allen.

After the ceremony, the Americans prepared to distribute government goods to Captain Jack and his people. These were the additional goods they would have received had they remained on the reservation. This was in keeping with the treaty of 1864. Captain Jack and his people arranged themselves in three concentric semicircles—one of men with Captain Jack and the other leaders at the center, one of women, and one of children. They received blankets, clothes, and cloth. The blankets were of high quality, heavy woolen eight-pounders. Captain Jack got four of these, the other leaders two, everyone else got one, except for six small children who received half blankets. Among the women were Captain Jack's two wives—one who looked older than he did; the other a pretty girl still in her teens, just starting to show her pregnancy.

The white men also handed out food. The Modocs soon retired to their camp to have a feast, but not before a little squabbling broke out. The Indians were given butchered beef. The Modocs were disappointed that they had not been given the whole steer. They relished the head and even the feet, a taste overlooked by the American butchers.

The Modoc women felt they had been cheated out of a delicacy. It did not help that when the American butchers had been preparing the beef, Klamath women had carried off the "head and pluck," as the Americans called what they regarded as the inedible parts of the beef. The ignorant Americans had allowed the Klamaths to swindle the Modocs, or so the more excitable Modoc women loudly claimed.

Despite this minor squabble, Meacham was still ebullient as he paced the reservation watching all the activity—the children gathering wood, the men smoking, the women starting to prepare the feast. Gambling began. Meacham was delighted to see Klamaths mingling so easily among Modocs. He thought he even saw a few Klamath warriors wooing Modoc maids.

It was December 31, the end of 1869. As the sun set behind the mountain peak and dusk spread across the reservation in long shadows, the Americans built a huge bonfire and invited everyone to a "*cultus wa-wa*," a phrase Meacham translated as "a big free talk." As many as five or six hundred Indians came. Everyone was free to talk about whatever he pleased. The Americans, especially Meacham, wanted to turn the talk to American law and Christian religion.

Link River Jack was the first to speak. Captain Jack had great affection for this wise old Klamath man, cunning as a coyote. Meacham did not share that estimate. He thought of Link River as one who held the old cherished superstitious ways around him like a blanket in tatters. But this night Link River was trying to impress Meacham, or at least to flatter him.

"I have long heard of this religion of the white man. I have heard about the Holy Spirit coming to him. I wonder if it would ever come to my people. I am old, I cannot live long. Maybe it has come now. I feel like a new kind of fire is in my heart. Maybe you have brought this Holy Spirit."

This must have pleased Meacham. He remembered that Link River had been exposed to Christianity twenty years before, at the Methodist mission led by the renowned missionary A. F. Waller. He found it remarkable how much the old man had retained, even the identification of the Holy Spirit with fire. But Link River went on a little too long, and there was a faint whiff of mischief in his last words.

He spoke of the bad blood among the Klamath, Modoc, and the Snake. But now they are all like brothers. *Tyee* Meacham alone has achieved this, Link River insisted.

"No common man could do this. Maybe you are the Holy Spirit. When I was a young man, I saw a white man on his knee for the Holy Spirit to come. Maybe the Great Spirit sent you with it."

In the flickering light of the bonfire Meacham peered at the old man, trying to figure out if his leg was being pulled. He could tell nothing from the old man's look, nor from the impassive faces around the fire. The subject quickly changed from religion to science.

Another old man asked how the white man could predict the darkening of the sun. The Modocs believed that the world was a flat disk with its center on the east shore of Tule Lake. The world had started small, but had gradually been woven outward, like a tule basket or mat. But the sun, moon, and stars were mysterious objects that defied human explanation.

Confronted with eclipses, the Modocs and Klamaths told an old story. Bear, always hungry, tried now and then to swallow Moon or Sun—but Frog chased him away by pissing on him, while the Modocs and Klamaths shouted their encouragement. How could the white man predict when Bear would swallow and Frog would piss?

So the whites explained to the Indians about the solar system. The old man said he now understood about eclipses, but Meacham doubted he was telling the truth, just being polite.

In this manner the big talk meandered on pleasantly, until one American noted that the year would be ending shortly. This excited the Indians. How could the Americans possibly know this? Meacham rose and showed his watch. He explained that when the two sticks were straight up the year would be over. David Allen pointed out that most of those around the fire could not even see the sticks. So for their benefit, would Meacham fire his pistol when the moment arrived?

After being assured the demonstration would not cause a panic, Meacham rose, held his pistol above his head. Shortly before midnight on December 31, 1869, he began the countdown, particularly pleased at the hushed silence in the crowd.

"Five minutes more and 1869 will be dead. . . . Four minutes now. . . . Now but three. . . . Two minutes more. . . . Now but one. . . ."

Then the flash of the gunshot and the report echoed up the canyons.

All the men around the bonfire shouted once, and all the Indians then shouted again. Meacham noticed that the Indians first shouted facing the west and then turned to shout facing the east, as if to bid good-bye to 1869 and then to bid welcome to 1870. Perhaps it was also to see if this particular death and birth produced anything noticeable at all in the sky. Or perhaps it was just hoping that Frog, even with Bear safely hibernating, would have a good piss across the night.

The crowd quickly dispersed, leaving behind at the smoldering fire just six men. Meacham and his interpreter; Captain Jack and David Allen; and two aged chiefs, Ocheo of the Paiute Snakes and Old Schonchin, once so feared. Old Schonchin, in particular, was an impressive sight, his face highlighted by the dying fire, his long gray hair buffeted by the brisk midnight winds.

Old Schonchin had been the great war chief when the Modocs were terrorizing wagon trains along the Applegate Trail. His explanation of his decision to lead his people onto the reservation was famous:

"I thought if we killed all the white men we saw, that no more would come. We killed all we could, but they came, more and more like the new grass in the spring. I looked around and saw that many of the young men were dead and could not come back to fight. My heart was sick. I threw down my gun. I said, 'I will not fight again.' I made friends with the white man."

Now Old Schonchin was standing beside A. B. Meacham, who felt he had done his best to complete the work of peace begun by this old warrior. He knew he would never forget that night. What he did not know was that he had not witnessed the beginning of a new age for the Modocs. Instead he had just made himself a central character in the first act of a Modoc tragedy.

2

I F THERE WAS a godly figure presiding at a distance over the Modoc tragedy it was William Tecumseh Sherman, destroyer of Georgia, implacable, incorruptible, the general who held the fate of the Amerian Indians in his bony hands. President Ulysses Grant had entrusted it to his old fellow commander, had handed it to him when he named him head of the army, or so Sherman believed.

News of Captain Jack's return to the Klamath reservation was welcomed in Washington, D.C., by Sherman, but not because he approved of the peace policy pursued by the likes of A. B. Meacham. Sherman was convinced that a general Indian war in the West was inevitable. To some admiring Yale students who called on him, he offered a prophecy: "I tell you that before you pass from the stage there will be fighting, in comparison with which mine will seem slight, and I have had enough."

Sherman's look backed his words. The Civil War had made him an old man at forty-six, old before his time. He had always been gaunt because of the asthma that often kept him awake at night wheezing and coughing. Now his reddish hair had grizzled into an unidentifiable, wavering hue. His scraggly beard darkened near the mouth where he always seemed to be working on the stub of a stogie. His flint eyes were still preternaturally alert. They observed everything with a disillusioned amusement that was revealed to be more than simple cynicism when that amusement suddenly shifted (as it often did these days) into fierce anger. Anyone who saw the transformation would be reminded that this was a man who had destroyed whole cities without a qualm.

Sherman's character was etched on his face. It was as if all the terrains he had traversed with his army had left their marks as lines and ridges. He had traversed too many of them to fit neatly on any map and so they had been chaotically superimposed upon one another. That face was the record of the price he had paid for all he had done. His men, despite his cadaverous appearance, still spoke of him affectionately as "Uncle Billy." But William Tecumseh Sherman knew for certain he wanted to be no one's Uncle Billy.

By the end of the war he had had his fill of public life, yet he had not managed to escape it. Southerners hated him as a merchant of terror, but in the North, people thought he was simply mad. One of his "insane" fits had led him to offer generous surrender terms to a prostrate enemy, so generous that his settlement had been summarily countermanded by the secretary of war. That was why, during the Grand Review of the victorious Union Army in Washington in May 1865, General Sherman had, in full view, pointedly snubbed Secretary Stanton. When the secretary of war offered his hand, Sherman ignored it and stiffly turned aside. His troops, seeing this, cheered him.

The general euphoria in Washington after the Civil War rankled Sherman. He particularly did not like being jostled by crowds of well-wishing civilians. He at one point had exploded, "Damn you, get out of the way, damn you," only to be met with the blithe question, "How about going to Mexico, General?" To this he had responded, not calmly, "You can go there if you like and you can go to hell if you want to!" Once again the press had fun with Crazy Sherman.

As soon as he could, he had fled westward. With his home in St. Louis, he thought of himself as a westerner. The Great Plains were to him like a great sea, with the settlements like little islands of civilization. Growing up in the West, he had concluded, was what made him so restless. He had looked forward to "take some years of cruising . . . to familiarize myself with all the interests and localities."

This he had done. From 1865 to 1868, he had been commander of the army division headquartered in St. Louis and had made the most of it, traveling constantly. As a consequence, he now felt he understood the military situation on the frontier as well as anyone. He saw it fundamentally as a military problem, and he consistently argued to superiors, such as Grant, that they should analyze it the same way.

Washington had been dealing with the Indians through the Department of the Interior. Even if the department's Indian agents were paragons of honesty (the general opinion was that most of them were crooked), their independence hobbled military commanders.

So Sherman complained to Grant in November 1865, "I am not even advised whether they [the Indians in his district] are to be localized, whether they are to have their hunting grounds guaranteed to them or indeed anything that would enable me to prejudge now, for our plans for protecting the whites must be modified to conform to these treaties."

His own plans for protecting the whites required them to behave sensibly. The army would guarantee protection to travelers only along certain specified routes; those who insisted on finding their own way west could do so at their own risk. He knew many wagon trains found tales of short cuts irresistible, but he did not care. "We must not be astonished if some of them lose their horses, cattle, and scalps."

He knew also that westerners themselves would become murderously outraged at the deaths of a few trespassing settlers, and that they usually expected the army to do the dirty work of satisfying their revenge lust. Journalists, moreover, could be counted upon to whip up the settlers by delivering incendiary editorials that compared Indians to wolves that had to be hunted down and exterminated once they had gotten the taste of blood.

What was going to happen in the long term, Sherman believed, should be obvious to anyone with two bits' worth of intelligence. The interests of the American settlers and the Indian tribes were fundamentally at odds. The Americans in the West already outnumbered the Indians by more than ten to one. The railroads would only increase that disparity, bringing to an end the era when the nomadic tribes of the Great Plains could follow the buffalo herds. This inevitable reckoning had been delayed while the American republic distracted itself with the issues of slavery and secession—but, in retrospect, the Indians were doomed once the Gold Rush of 1849 made California a state and America securely a transcontinental republic.

So the Indian tribes had to be localized—collected on reservations like the one that had lumped the Klamaths, the Modocs, and the Snakes into their state of enforced togetherness. In Sherman's view, those Indians who did not wish to adjust peaceably had to be threatened and pressured "to freeze and starve a little more, I reckon, before they listen to common sense." Those who remained implacable had to be killed. It was as simple as that. The more clearly this reality was seen, and the more consistently and resolutely it was acted upon, the less loss of life there would be on both sides.

Reconstruction was working in the South only where Southerners admitted they had lost the Civil War, once and for all. The reconstruction of the western Indians would work only where Indians recognized that they were losing the war for the West, once and for all. To give them hope of any other possible outcome might be well intentioned, but it was cruelty of the worst kind.

Enforcing the policy required ruthlessness. No one in his right mind would want to witness, let alone be responsible for, the inevitable slaughter. So Sherman consistently argued that any young man who had the slightest prospects in civilian life should stay out of the army.

Given the situation, Sherman had his doubts about prominent military men of the younger generation attracted to frontier service. George Armstrong Custer, for instance, he thought "young, very brave even to brashness, a good trait for a Cavalry officer . . . [but] he has not too much sense."

Although Sherman was generally lionized whenever he visited frontier towns, he was no lover of the settlers. They, of course, were continually pleading with him for an army fort near their towns. But he usually found that "the size of Indian stampedes and scares diminishes as I approach their location." As often as not these towns were using the Indians not to get army protection but to get army business. "All the people west of the Missouri River look to the Army as their legitimate field of profit & support," he wrote in 1866, "and the quicker they are undeceived the better for all."

Although the settlers systematically exaggerated the danger from Indians, what Sherman had taken to calling "these awful distances" made it virtually impossible to respond effectively to real Indian attacks. The commander never tired of pointing out that his division in St. Louis was responsible for a region 1,000 miles long and more than 1,300 miles wide—impossible to control. Thus there was sure to be a lengthy period of ugly hostilities between the two peoples, with much suffering and loss of life on both sides. Ignoring this reality would only prolong the suffering and increase the loss of life.

That, of course, was exactly what the politicians were trying to do, backed by a chorus of earnest idealists. These good hearts pretended to believe, and some fools may really have believed, that the Indian question could be resolved by a series of treaties. Had these people never read any history? Did they not realize that treaties were kept only as long as they were in the interests of both parties?

Treaties would be kept on the American side only until the Americans wanted Indian land, and then the American government would find it lacked the will to enforce its own word. The Indians, for their part, behaved no better. They signed and broke treaties whenever it suited them. "They will sign any treaty for the sake of the annuities," Sherman wrote, "but can no more fill their part of the contract than if it were waste paper. There is a universal feeling of distrust on both sides, and this will sooner or later result in a general outbreak." Told of chiefs who claimed their young men were uncontrollable, he responded: "Tell the rascals so are mine; and if another white man is scalped in all this region, it will be impossible to hold mine in."

Despite his bleak outlook, Sherman enjoyed the West, the long trips in the field, the spinning of yarns around the campfire, the sense of building something that would endure. Nation building was much better than just destroying, no matter how noble the cause. He foresaw horrible fights, but the outcome in the West would be a stable and prosperous American society.

From 1865 to 1868 William Tecumseh Sherman, one suspects, was as happy as someone of his perceptions and disposition can be.

In 1868 General Ulysses S. Grant was elected president, an inevitability that Sherman welcomed for the republic almost as much as he dreaded it for himself. The post of General of the Army was now open, and Sherman knew he was almost certain to be tapped. That meant moving to Washington, a place Sherman considered "corrupt as hell," one he hoped to avoid "like the pest house." Once the election was over, Sherman determined not to go to Washington unless Grant ordered him there. He even hoped for his own sake that the Congress might decide to do without a General of the Army.

He did his best to stir up opposition against his appointment. In one indiscreet diatribe leaked to the press on November 30, 1868, he ridiculed those who thought the army wanted war with the Indians. The military wanted only to finish an inevitable war, not to start one.

"If it results in the utter annihilation of these Indians, it is but the result of what they have been warned again and again, and for which they seem fully prepared. I will say nothing and do nothing to restrain our troops from doing what they deem proper on the spot, and will allow no more vague charges of cruelty and inhumanity to tie their hands."

When testifying before the Senate in January 1869, he was utterly defiant. If the country and its political leaders persisted in regarding the Indian question as something other than a military problem, "I am absolved from all responsibility and will simply say 'Farewell Mr. Indian,' for you know he is doomed. You will need a stronger Army than ever to protect the Indian against citizens who will rescue their stolen horses and will avenge on innocent and guilty the loss of their families."

Then Grant, as expected, asked Sherman to become head of the army; and Sherman, also as expected, reluctantly acquiesced. Not long after he accepted, however, he realized that he had made a grave mistake. He knew he would hate Washington and its politicians. What he discovered only too late was that his old comrade-in-arms Ulysses S. Grant had become a pliable part of that world. Grant was not going to support Sherman's policies in the West. This took Sherman almost completely by surprise, even though he thought himself long past being surprised by anything or anyone. It was as if he had led an Army of the West into an ambush. It was a lapse of judgment as infuriating as it was unforgivable.

Grant's inaugural address on March 4, 1869, was carefully noncommittal on the Indian question: "The proper treatment of the original occupants of the land—the Indians—is one deserving of careful study. I will favor any course toward them which tends to their civilization and ultimate citizenship."

No one in Washington, including Sherman, could disagree with that statement, nor could anyone find anything to cheer in it.

The next day Grant accepted Sherman's price for accepting the unwanted position of General of the Army: he would have a free hand to run the army as he saw fit. Here were the orders: "The chiefs of staff corps, departments and bureaus will report to and act under the immediate orders of the general commanding the Army. All official business, which by law or regulations require the action of the President or Secretary of War, will be submitted by the General of the Army to the Secretary of War, and, in general, all orders from the President or Secretary of War to any portion of the Army, line or staff, will be transmitted through the General of the Army."

But this arrangement lasted less than a month. Then Grant called Sherman in to tell him face-to-face that his secretary of war "feels badly" about Sherman's autonomy, and Grant did not want to upset the secretary further since his health was not well.

"So, Sherman," Grant added, "you'll have to publish a rescinding order."

Letting Sherman himself issue the order was Grant's feeble attempt to let Sherman save face. But Sherman would not be mollified. He asked pointedly what Grant thought the general response would be to this sudden change.

Grant responded absently, "Well, if it's my own order, I can rescind it, can't I?"

Sherman immediately stood up, at something close to mock attention. With formal precision, he said, "Yes, Mr. President, you have the power to revoke your own order; you shall be obeyed. Good morning, sir."

For the rest of that spring Sherman watched his influence over Western policy dissolve. Grant, after vacillating, adopted a "Quaker policy" that delegated the primary responsibility for the Indians to religious leaders. The Methodists were given Oregon, hence the appointment of A. B. Meacham.

The turnabout came even though Grant, in principle, agreed with Sherman about the West. The president had written in 1866 that the transfer of Indian Affairs from the Department of the Interior to the War Department was a "matter of first importance." Congress, however, liked the patronage spoils that Indian affairs offered. An Indian agency was a lucrative plum to have on hand to reward important supporters back home. Besides, Congress did not want Grant to be able to use Indian affairs to justify keeping a large number of high-ranking officers in the army, or at least in government service.

For the moment, Grant decided he could not, or would not, fight Congress on this point, but he did take his own revenge. In Sherman's hearing, he told congressional leaders, "Gentlemen, you have defeated my plans of Indian management; but you will not succeed in your purpose, for I will divide these appointments up among religious churches, with which you dare not contend."

Sherman relished the effectiveness of Grant's revenge. He now thought, however, that the West was in even worse hands than before. Putting idealistic religious reformers in charge of the Indian question, rather than using corrupt political appointees, might be a temporary improvement, but it still fell far short of Sherman's military solution. Sherman, as a consequence, became even more outspoken in his criticisms.

In 1870 Sherman, along with other notables such as Secretary of the Interior Delano, sent greetings to be read to the delegates of an advocacy group calling itself the "United States Indian Commission." The tone of Sherman's note was in marked contrast to the platitudinous praise of the others. After introductory pleasantries, he wrote:

> I doubt not the generous feelings of the good people interested in the meeting but it does seem to me that they accomplish little or no good. The Indian question is a practical one, and not one of mere feeling; and so far as my observation extends, the wild Indians are rather harmed than benefited by the conflict of extreme opinion which the public meetings engender. The real question can only be discussed fairly where the Indians are, and if you will adjourn your meeting to Fort Sully, Fort Rice, or Fort Fetterman, where you can see Indians themselves, I will feel strongly inclined to attend the adjourned meeting.

The audience sat stunned and in silence. Then an influential delegate, the Quaker Lucretia Coffin Mott of Philadelphia, rose to ask to have the letter read again. After the second reading, she angrily said Sherman had "proved himself false to humanity by sending such a contemptuous letter." Others quickly joined in the condemnation. Had Sherman been present, he would have heartily enjoyed the uproar, mutual contempt serving him always as a tonic.

Contempt would certainly have been the general's attitude to A. B. Meacham's idealism, but at least this do-gooder was in the field, dealing with real Indians who one day might actually kill him. Unlike those sitting comfortably in New York, Meacham was putting his scalp where his mouth was. At any rate, Sherman could only be grateful that things were temporarily quiet on the California–Oregon border. Things were anything but quiet in Arizona, where the Apaches were once again making themselves prime candidates for extermination. Sherman had to order his best troops in the Pacific Northwest, under the leadership of General Crook, to the Southwest. His own view was that Arizona and New Mexico were more trouble than they were worth and that the United States ought to loan Mexico money to buy them back.

This transfer of troops left the California–Oregon border vulnerable, but there was no choice in such a vast war of skirmishes, especially when each year Congress reduced the size of the army. A standing army of 54,000 had been cut to 30,000 in just a few years. Thus in the West Sherman had to rob Peter to pay Paul. He could only hope that Meacham had judged the situation correctly.

Three months later, Sherman learned that Captain Jack had left the reservation once again—this time with four hundred followers. What the General of the Army said has been mercifully left unrecorded by history.

3

AT FIRST everything had seemed fine on the Klamath reservation. Jack's Modocs had set to work to build what looked as though it would be a permanent settlement. They had reconciled with the reservation Modocs led by Old Schonchin.

Then the Klamaths started treating the Modocs like mendicants living on the Klamath dole. Just when the needling started is unknown. Apparently it was started by Link River Jack, whose mischievous sense of humor Captain Jack relished when it was directed at others. Now Link River Jack and the other Klamaths began to address each Modoc they encountered as "Stranger." They then reminded the Modocs that they were only guests on Klamath land. Looking at a pile of lumber, they would say blandly, "It is our timber; you may use it, but it is ours. You can make rails, but we want some of them." When Captain Jack and others bridled, the Klamaths responded with benign condescension, never violating the letter of the treaty, constantly perverting its spirit.

Finally Captain Jack and his people could stand no more, and he appealed to the local reservation agent, Captain O. C. Knapp (Meacham's headquarters were in Salem, more than two hundred miles away). Knapp saw his assignment as a dead-end post: he was simply waiting until something better turned up. As Meacham put it, "Knapp came to the work having no heart in it." A place server in the worst sense, he thought he had discharged his obligations to the Indians when he issued rations to them on schedule. Beyond that he wished them to trouble him as little as possible.

Discussions with Captain Jack, Knapp did not need to be told, could only mean trouble; so he attempted to forestall him. Seeing Captain Jack approach his office, Knapp did not wait for him to enter but intercepted him outside. After listening to the Modocs' complaints, he did his best to brush him off with assurances that he would make things right, then he told Captain Jack to get on with his work.

Knapp did nothing to straighten out the problem, however. Captain Jack did return to his work, and the Klamath returned to their needling they were getting quite good at, thanks to plenty of practice. So once again Captain Jack intruded upon Knapp's tranquillity. The second time Knapp suggested that Captain Jack move his people away from the Link River Klamaths. He suggested a point on the Williamson River, a few miles closer to the agency.

Captain Jack followed Knapp's advice, and soon his people were starting to build new lodges on the point. Then the Klamaths nearest to the new Modoc settlement learned of Link River Jack's amusing game, and they took up the taunting. "You can stay here; but it is our country." "Your horses can eat the grass; but it is Klamath grass." "You can catch fish; but they belong to us." "You can use this, but don't forget that it is all ours."

Yet again Captain Jack broke into Knapp's relaxation. This time Knapp made no secret of his exasperation. Captain Jack could move again, but the next time he had better stay moved. Captain Jack at last concluded that Knapp was going to be of no help. The situation, despite the promises of Meacham and David Allen, was only going to get worse.

Move again? Jack knew no place on the Klamath reservation that he liked so well as those he was being driven from. If he was going to move and stay moved, there was only one place for him and his people to go. But it wasn't on the reservation. The Modocs should return to Smiles of God.

Captain Jack called a secret meeting of the Modocs. Almost all came, not just those who had left the reservation earlier. Captain Jack denounced Knapp as a man who had no heart for them, was probably a bad man, and certainly would not keep the superintendent's promises. Speaking for himself, Captain Jack said he had no intention of living any longer on Klamath land; he would live on Modoc land where he belonged. He was leaving the reservation again, this time for good. He concluded, "Who will go with me? Who wants to stay with a man who has no heart for us?"

Meacham later learned of this meeting from Tobey Riddle's brother, who was there and who tried to argue against Captain Jack. The meeting had been long and stormy, but Captain Jack had prevailed. Having led less than one hundred Modocs back to the reservation, Captain Jack now led more than four hundred out. So many went that even Old Schonchin had to join them or become a headman without a tribe.

The return of the Modocs to Tule Lake alarmed the struggling settlers nearby, but their reappearance in Yreka was the occasion for celebration. The situation in Modoc territory had been changing rapidly since the original treaty of 1864. As Ivan Applegate put it, "Nearly every foot of it fit for cultivation has been taken up by settlers whose thousands of cattle, horses and sheep are ranging over it." Applegate doubted that the Modoc could support themselves.

Although they could not support themselves for much of the year according to the traditional ways, many Modoc men had become skilled at handling livestock. Large ranches to the west of their territory near Hot Creek offered jobs, and a band of the Modocs settled there. John Fairchild and Pressly Dorris, two ranchers, were eager to hire Modocs as hands.

Others looking for temporary work could find it in Yreka, where women might find temporary husbands. One local judge, A. M. Roseborough, even provided Captain Jack with what amounted to a letter of introduction informing newcomers "who are not acquainted with him he is friendly . . . and always had been friendly to whites." The settlers in southern Oregon and around Tule Lake, however, showed no sign of being comforted by a character reference from Yreka.

Meacham thought he understood the enthusiasm of Yreka for Captain Jack and his band: avarice. "The Modoc trade may have had something to do with the success of more than one merchant in Yreka." He added disdainfully, "What more natural than the fact that the dissolute portion of the Yreka people should espouse the Modoc cause, and that the better part of society should form their opinions from stories circulated by friends?"

The Indian agent was stung by stories, repeated earnestly by Yrekans, that the Modocs had been starved off the reservation by a corrupt administration. He tried to forgive Captain Jack and his band for being the source of the stories. He even drew a moral from the gossip. "Mankind are prone to be swayed in the direction of self-interest," he reflected. "When encouraged, any poor mortal may tell a falsehood so often that he really believes it to be true."

The agent, however, was going to do more than wistfully moralize. When Knapp retired soon after the Modocs returned to Tule Lake, Meacham had him replaced with someone he could be sure would carry out his directives: John Meacham, his brother. He knew he had to do something about the insufferable taunts of the Klamaths, so he decided to establish a semiautonomous reservation nine miles to the west of the main one, at a place called Yainax, where traditionally the Klamaths and Modocs had come together as equals. What Meacham undoubtedly did not know was that Yainax had served as a slave market for the two peoples.

Meacham assigned the new settlement its own agent, Ivan Applegate, who had helped Meacham when he coaxed Captain Jack back to the reservation before. Applegate knew as much as anyone about the Indians of this region, and he had the backing of the formidable Applegate clan. Meacham also moved the Snakes who were on the Klamath reservation to Yainax, though he created the Yainax reservation primarily to lure Captain Jack and the Modocs by assuring them they would no longer have to put up with Klamath insults.

A brilliant move, or so it seemed at first. Soon Old Schonchin went to Yainax with a hundred or so of his supporters. Captain Jack visited the new reservation and talked as if he were considering settling there himself. Then Modoc tradition introduced its own complication.

In June one of Captain Jack's nieces became seriously ill while Curley Headed Doctor was away (on a horse-stealing expedition, according to one account). Captain Jack sought help from a Klamath shaman, Comptowas, who was so confident he could cure the child he took payment in advance. Then the child died.

As the Modoc saw it, Comptowas, in taking advanced payment, had shown that the case was not a difficult one. Obviously he could have cured the child if he had chosen to. Instead he had chosen to let her die, even to kill her. How typical of the Klamath, professing friendship and then using their advantage to harm the Modoc! Captain Jack had Comptowas executed, an act fully justified within both Klamath and Modoc traditions. In these cultures, to be a shaman was a dangerous profession.

The Yrekans saw things entirely from Captain Jack's point of view. Elijah Steele, with Roseborough, the other judge in the town, expressed a common opinion: "The white people should not meddle with them [the Modocs] in their laws among themselves, further than to try to persuade them out of such foolish notions. White people here are not mad at them for executing their own laws, and should not be anywhere."

The Oregon settlers near the Modocs saw the execution as a cold-blooded murder—proof, if any were needed, that Captain Jack and his people had to be herded back onto the reservation. Superstitions made the Indians entirely unpredictable. Who knew when their traditions would dictate the killing of a settler or the kidnapping of children? Whatever the case, Captain Jack was guilty of cold-blooded murder pure and simple, and white justice demanded he be punished.

The legal situation was in fact a little more difficult than the more sympathetic Yrekans wished to admit. Because Captain Jack had signed the treaty of 1864, he was, from the federal government's point of view, a reservation Indian. As a result, American law did apply to him.

Therefore Ivan Applegate, from the Yainax reservation, felt compelled to request formally that the sheriff of Siskiyou County (of which Yreka was the seat) arrest Captain Jack and four others implicated in the death of Compotwas. Somehow the sheriff never got around to it, although Captain Jack and his men seemed to be going in and out of Yreka all the time. An army platoon was then sent to Yreka to see what it could do. It returned having done nothing. The Yreka newspaper praised Captain Jack and his men for helping put out a fire in the town during the Fourth of July celebrations, exactly when the platoon should have been in town as well.

The military report on the episode was succinct but embarrassed. The Modocs were "insolent beggars." The failure to arrest Captain Jack was due to the interference of Yreka "squaw men." As for Captain Jack's own whereabouts, opinions in Yreka were "very conflicting."

The settlers, in contrast, were of one mind. They saw the annoying, even threatening presence of the Modocs, the collusion of Yreka, the inaction and incompetence and indifference of the government, taken together or separately, as an indefensible affront to life, liberty, and the pursuit of American happiness. Jesse Applegate, uncle of Ivan and with two sons among the settlers, decided to act as the advocate of their interests. So he wrote to Meacham.

The Modocs had become "very saucy." The widely scattered settlers and their property were at "the mercy of the marauders." "A state of terrorism" had fallen upon the settlers. All this Meacham had heard before. He discounted it.

Applegate insisted on placing the most ominous interpretation on Modoc sauciness. After a careful reconnaissance of the region, he had become convinced the Modocs were preparing for all-out war:

"They have concealed their non-combatants in some unknown retreat, & the men of the band, fully armed, in parties of 10 or 15, rove over the settlements declaring their intention to fight the soldiers should they come to arrest Captain Jack, and living well upon the charity of the settlers which is much improved by the fear the Indians inspire."

Applegate urged Meacham to realize that the situation was "extremely critical and needs your prompt attention." Just a single violent act from one imprudent or panicky settler could involve the whole region "in all the horrors of an Indian War, & many valuable lives may be lost and property destroyed before even so small a band as that of Capt. Jack is brought into subjection or exterminated." As for himself, he was returning to the region to be near his sons, to "render any assistance if attacked."

How much Meacham believed of this is hard to say, perhaps about as much as he believed of the rosy reports about Captain Jack regularly issued from Yreka. Meacham could concede readily that the Modocs were annoying the settlers. The Modocs reminded them constantly that they were living on Modoc land. They would also occasionally demand token payment, a little hay perhaps or some food. When Modoc women found a dead cow on the range, they butchered it immediately for themselves, not respecting white ownership. The Modoc men had a knack for showing up at settlers' cabins when the men were away, thereby frightening the women and children. But from the Modoc point of view they were doing nothing more to the settlers than what the Klamaths had done to Modocs back at the reservation.

Nonetheless, Jesse Applegate was a respected and influential man, and his nephew was Meacham's hand-picked assistant at Yainax. The situation was touchy, if not critical. Applegate's dire analysis required action to calm the settlers. So Meacham, who was tied up with another negotiation elsewhere, decided to send his brother to the Modocs as his emissary, along with Ivan Applegate. "You can say to them that you represent me—my heart, my wishes, my words; and that I have authorized you to talk for me." They should believe this since they knew John was his brother.

Meacham directed his brother to make an offer to Captain Jack and his people. The Indian agent no longer wanted them to go to Yainax for good. He made them a promise: "I will try to get a small reserve for them in their country. . . . I will lay the whole matter before the department at Washington, and put it through if possible." This, he warned them, would take time—and in the meantime he would prefer that they wait at the Klamath reservation or Yainax. He further promised that Captain Jack and the others would be free, at least temporarily, from any repercussions for the murder of the Klamath shaman.

Meacham in his orders to his brother could not resist adding an exhortation: "Go on this mission realizing that you carry in your hand the lives and happiness of many persons, and the salvation of a tribe of people who have been much wronged, and seldom, if ever, understood."

The meeting was arranged and held on Ivan Applegate's ranch on August 21, 1870. The arrangements specified that Captain Jack was to appear with only a few men, and everyone was to come unarmed. Captain Jack, however, brought many warriors, and they were all armed. Before the negotiations could begin, John Meacham and Applegate had to listen to a harangue in Modoc by Black Jim, Captain Jack's dark-skinned brother, ostensibly to them but obviously directed primarily to Captain Jack himself. When the gist of the talk was translated for them, they learned that Black Jim had denounced any negotiations with the whites.

Despite the ominous beginning, the subsequent negotiations could scarcely have been more cordial. Captain Jack was apologetic about the killing, but it was only self-defense. What was to prevent this shaman from using his powers to poison others of his family? The Modoc insisted that he would not return to the reservation, but assured Meacham and Applegate that he and his people had no malicious designs on the settlers. He was pleased with the proposal for a new reservation.

John Meacham reported to his brother, "Permit me to assure you that there is no danger at present of any serious trouble between the Modoc Indians and the settlers."

Meacham was satisfied that the fears of the settlers were un-grounded, although he did not tell them that. The settlers, however, saw through him. The migrating water birds had left Tule Lake, winter frosts had started, and the snows would come soon. Now was the time for military action against Captain Jack, yet nothing was being done.

The settlers realized they themselves had to do something or be stuck with the band for another year, since everyone knew the Modocs could only be removed during the winter, when they were most vulner-able. As one settler put it, "As well expect to collect coyotes out of that region of rock, mountain and morass as the Indians in the summer sea-son." He added, by way of explanation, that when the Modoc could live off the land "no kind of force can pursue as fast as they can retreat, and the [whole] military force in the Pacific is insufficient to hunt them out and rout them in their fastness."

The settlers began a prolonged petition campaign in January 1871. One petition, signed by more than forty settlers, was sent to Meacham, to be forwarded to the military. Another was sent to the governor of Oregon. These were supplemented by individual letters. The flavor of these petitions can be adequately represented by a sin-gle, long line to the governor:

> They frequently watching the men leave their House & insulted the femail inmates of our sacred Homes; And they Boast Defiance, to the Authorities to whoome we the undersigned freaquantly at least one Dozen times, through Petiation, & otherwise The Militarys, hands are tide By Orders they are Kean to extend the Disird protection, but are subject to the Superintendants Orders, and he has turnd the Deaf yeare to protestations from us, and lets the Indians go on with theire menicing work.

This particular petition concluded with the implied threat that the settlers were about to take matters into their own hands, and then the military would have no choice but to intervene. Or, as the petition put it,

"Forebearance had allmost ceast to be a virtue." When will the trouble start? "Shurley soon if something is not promtley don to protect us."

Another, more literate settler wrote, "They have come to my place and fired into my barn, knowing there were men in it at the time. They have torn down my fences and turned their stock into my fields. Armed parties have come here and made hostile demonstrations, causing fear in the minds of myself and the people here. They have stated to me that they claim the Lost River country and if the white man wants the water and grass he will have to pay for it."

After an entire year of these letters, A. B. Meacham finally succumbed to the pressure. He might still trust Captain Jack's good intentions, but those good intentions were worthless if the settlers started something. Then the bellicose members of Captain Jack's band would dictate policy, and general war would ensue. On January 25, 1872, Meacham wrote to the military commander of the Columbia District asking to have Jack and his people returned, forcibly if necessary, to the reservation: "I regret very much the necessity of this action, but the peace and welfare of white settlers and Indians demand that it be done promptly."

The future of the Modocs was now the immediate responsibility of General E. R. S. Canby.

Canby had been in charge of the Department of Columbia since 1870, a command that included all the troops in Oregon, Washington, and Idaho. He had been sent by Sherman to replace General Crook after the earlier trouble with Captain Jack was resolved and Crook could be spared for the Southwest. Canby was well suited to a quiet tour in a remote command. In the eyes of Washington he had more than earned it.

A plain-faced man—large nose, deep-set eyes, and floppy ears—Canby looked, in an early photograph, a little like a clean-shaven version of a more famous native Kentuckian, Abraham Lincoln. A West Pointer, Canby, now fifty-two, had never quite distinguished himself. Although he received two decorations for gallantry during the Mexican War, he was really more a staff officer than a field commander. He had spent most of the Civil War in Washington, D.C., and had taken over the command of New York City after the draft riots in 1863. The end of the war found him as a general commanding his own army in southern Mississippi. He was credited with having taken Mobile, Mississippi. His Civil War had almost ended prematurely, and somewhat embarrassingly. While reconnoitering the river he was shot through the buttocks by a sniper; he seems to have supervised much of the siege of Mobile lying down.

Canby was a popular officer, perhaps because he was so obviously a limited one both in talent and ambition. The general was as homely in mind as he was in face—straightforward, plodding, unimaginative, humorless, and apparently oblivious to the human complexities that had been President Lincoln's native ground. Canby's classmates at West Point had liked and respected him. As ambitious, aspiring classmates such as Henry Halleck and Tecumseh Sherman (both of whom had also served with Canby in California during the Gold Rush) rose to eminence within the army, they looked after the career of the reliable, by-the-book Canby. Contemporaries called Canby "prudent."

During the difficult years after the war he had been of much use to Washington. He served in one impossible assignment after another in the South during Reconstruction. He followed orders, kept his word, and was never vindictive. Southerners, not surprisingly, hated him anyway. One Virginian called his administration "as brutish a tyranny as ever marked the course of any government whose agents and organs claimed it to be civilized." This irrational rancor left Canby, who was only doing the best he could, saddened and perplexed and, in the end, spent. He needed a simpler assignment, one as far away from the scenes of the recent war as he could get. His friends in the army took care of him once again.

The Department of the Columbia was a command of 1,225 men. The force was far weaker, however, than the number suggested. The best troops were regularly transferred to the Southwest, to fight Apaches. The rest were prone to desertion, more than two hundred a year. Canby did his best to shore up his understaffed forts and to arrange appointments, transfers, promotions, requisitions. A bureaucrat with epaulets, he liked to absorb himself in humdrum details. He was even adjusting to the drizzly weather of the Northwest as a welcome change from the tropical heat of Washington and the Deep South.

Now trouble was boiling up at the southernmost extent of his command, trouble that was spilling over into the territory of the California Department, the other major command of the Pacific Division. Canby preferred to do as little as possible—and, before doing even that, to check with his superiors. Still, he was a man who knew his duty and prided himself on having never shirked it.

This situation around Tule Lake was, according to the reports and petitions Canby was receiving from others, deteriorating. The Modocs were not just stealing and engaging in petty extortion; they had begun to threaten the lives of settlers. Canby found himself being informed that this border region was "on the verge of a desolating Indian war." One dispatch asked rhetorically, "Shall a petty Indian chief with twenty desperadoes and a squalid band of three hundred miserable savages any longer set at defiance the strong arm of the Government, driving our citizens from our homes, threatening their lives and destroying their property?"

The reports were undoubtedly full of exaggerations. Canby was experienced enough in dealing with civilians to know that. No white settlers had been forcibly driven from their homes, although a number of residents in and about Linkville claimed to have been scared away from their homesteads when Captain Jack had led his people out of the reservation in 1869. Nonetheless, Meacham seemed rattled. He caved in and decided to reverse his earlier policy of accommodation before it had been given time to work.

Canby replied to Meacham's request for military action with careful reasoning based on legalistic distinctions. He knew that Meacham had already reached a temporary settlement with Captain Jack and his band. Both sides were now waiting for the decision of Washington on a new Modoc reservation in the Tule Lake region. Moving troops into this territory would constitute an obvious violation of the temporary agreement, and thereby put at risk the whole settlement that Meacham had so effectively negotiated. Arresting Captain Jack and the other leaders would be tantamount to a declaration of war. The request for troops was denied.

Canby went out of his way to express sympathy for the Modoc position, writing: "I am not surprised at the unwillingness of the Modocs to return to any point on the reservation where they would be exposed to the hostilities and annoyances they have hitherto experienced (and without adequate protection) from the Klamath." He also obliquely suggested that Meacham and other reservation officials may have outlived their usefulness: "With their imperfect reasoning powers, and natural suspicions, they [the Modocs] have concluded that they were intentionally deceived and now distrust the agents of the Indian Department."

Not surprisingly, the always careful Canby sought and got the support of his superior, the commander of the whole Pacific Division, Major General J. M. Schofield, for his decision to deny the request for troops.

This response stunned Meacham. The man of peace requests troops from the man of war. And the man of war, rather than addressing the substance of the request, scores debating points. Canby was behaving more like a bureaucrat than a general. But Meacham did not lose his temper; he tried to reason with Canby on his own terms. He argued that the Modocs had already rendered the temporary agreement null and void. So he wrote to Canby in a letter dated February 8, 1872: "Had they behaved honestly, and on their part maintained peaceable relations with the white settlers, they might have remained at Modoc Lake undisturbed. Such has not been the case, and much as I regret the necessity for forcible arrest and return to the reservation, I can see no other way to secure peace and mete out justice."

Jesse Applegate, perhaps with Meacham's encouragement, also waded in, as usual putting the worst face on things: the Modocs "have misunderstood your forbearance and humanity, and think your policy dictated by weakness and fear, and the impunity with which they commit aggressions and levy 'black mail' upon the settlers encourages and confirm that belief." He added caustically that if the humanitarians who now controlled Indian policy had the interests of the Modoc truly at heart they would remove them from a situation that put them as much at risk as the settlers.

Canby ignored Meacham's second request. Two weeks later Meacham tried again. The occasion for his new letter was intelligence that "the settlers are making preparation for self-defense." Did Canby not understand the urgency of the situation? Effective actions could be taken against Captain Jack's band only during the winter.

This continued pressure could not have pleased Canby, who had come to regard the decision on honoring the temporary agreement to be Washington's—not Meacham's, not his. In early April, Washington decided. The Modocs were to be removed, and so was A. B. Meacham. The Indian superintendent was to blame for the failure of the temporary agreement.

T. B. Odeneal, Meacham's successor, knew nothing of the Modocs and cared less. He had served earlier with the Osages, and he professed to support the peace policy. But he also liked to talk tough, this predilection covering up for a genuine timidity. T. B. Odeneal was scared of Indians.

He must have realized almost immediately that he was the wrong person to deal with the nettled Modocs. No sooner had he assumed his new position than he wanted out as quickly as possible, though with his good name intact—and no one quite realized how much his responsibilities frightened him. As Indian superintendent, Odeneal would talk tough but look for excuses to stay as far away from Indians as possible. This meant, in practice, finding ways to put other people in danger.

Odeneal wrote in 1873 that he knew exactly the mistake made by his predecessor A. B. Meacham:

> The jaw-bone policy is, in my estimation, the source of more trouble with the Indians than anything else. Too much "pow wow" is the prime cause of trouble with Jack, who has a remarkable faculty of misconstruing everything said to suit his own purposes, and then claiming that bad faith has been practiced. A little prompt action and less talk, when he first left the reservation before he had become emboldened by repeated successes in "pow wowing" would have accomplished the desired object.

Opposing the "jaw-bone" had a convenient corollary. Odeneal refused to talk with Captain Jack, lest Captain Jack conclude that the superintendent was someone who would yield to the Modoc whims. Insisting that the Modocs be dealt with firmly meant military action, with T. B. Odeneal rooting for the soldiers from a safe distance. He also quickly realized that if things went sour he could conveniently blame the men of Yreka as well as Meacham for any trouble. Oregonians were quick to believe any bad report about their southern compatriots.

Odeneal did have to face one difficulty. Military operations against the Modocs would have to wait until the following winter. The superintendent, therefore, had to get through the better part of a year, appearing to be doing something to resolve the situation peaceably while being particularly careful never to put himself in harm's way.

The obvious thing to do was to jaw-bone with Captain Jack to see if his position had softened. Odeneal decided—for reasons he never specified—that it was "impracticable" to go to Captain Jack's camp himself. Instead, he sent Applegate out to the village in May. He returned to report Captain Jack's words to the superintendent, who had as yet never laid eyes upon him. Odeneal set them down:

> We are good people, and will not kill or frighten anybody. We want peace and friendship. I am well known and understood by the people of Yreka, California, and am governed by their advice. I do not want to live upon the reservation, for the Indians there are poorly clothed, suffer from hunger, and even have to leave the reservation sometimes to make a living. We are willing to have whites live in our country, but do not want them to locate on the west side and near the mouth of Lost River, where we have our winter camps. The settlers are continually lying about my people and trying to make trouble.

Captain Jack apparently had been thinking very concretely about a territorial adjustment to preserve the peace. Let the Modocs have the west side of Lost River and the site for their winter camp; the settlers could have the rest. True, the Modocs could not support themselves on so small a reservation, but Captain Jack had thought of that too. The men and boys could work for the Americans, as they had done before. The people of Yreka could attest to that. The women, children, and old men would live their traditional life on their ancestral lands.

This would have been a proposal worth discussing, had Odeneal been willing to talk to the Modoc leader face to face, had Odeneal not already decided that pow wows were the source of all the trouble. Or, as he would write later, had he not already decided that "Indians should be dealt with kindly and humanely, but more as if they were children than men, until they can be educated in the ways and habits of civilized life." You did not negotiate with children.

When Odeneal wrote in June to Washington, needless to say, he did not describe the Modocs as good people wanting peace and friendship.

Rather he found within this band, not childishness, but a full-fledged conspiracy of evil: "The leaders of these Indians are desperadoes, brave, daring and reckless—and their superior sagacity enables them to exercise full and complete control over the rest of the tribe. They have for so long a time been permitted to do as they please that they imagine they are too powerful to be controlled by the government, and that they can with impunity defy its authority. This, in my opinion, is the whole secret of their insubordination."

Odeneal's proposed course of action was to seize the Modoc leaders and hold them away from their band "until they shall agree to behave themselves." This proposal was quickly approved in Washington. It was now July. Odeneal had only to wait until full winter to initiate military action, and not even Canby could resist.

In November Odeneal asked Captain Jack and the other Modoc leaders, the very men he wanted arrested, to come parlay with him. He instructed his messenger, "Tell them that I entertain none but the most friendly feelings for them." Jack was not fooled. Once again, Odeneal recorded the words reported back to him.

"Say to the superintendent that we do not wish to see him, or to talk with him. We do not want any white men to tell us what to do. Our friends and counselors are men in Yreka, California. They tell us to stay where we are, and we intend to do it, and will not go to the reservation. I am tired of being talked to, and am done with talking."

This was just what Odeneal wanted to hear. He immediately requested from the commander of Fort Klamath "sufficient force to compel said Indians to camp Yainax, on Klamath Reservation." Odeneal could now wash his hands of the Modoc problem. "I transfer the whole matter to your department," he told the commander. He also sent out some men with vague orders to warn the settlers near the Modocs that hostilities might be imminent.

On November 27, 1872, Odeneal sent Ivan Applegate to Fort Klamath with his request for a military force to remove Captain Jack and his people to Yainax at once. He himself hunkered down in Linkville rather than risk a parlay with the Modoc leader. Applegate rode through the night and arrived at the fort at 5 A.M., Thursday, November 28, the morning of Thanksgiving. He was met by the sergeant of the guard who immediately brought him to Frazier Boutelle, a lieutenant who had risen through the ranks to captain during the Civil War, reverted to the ranks after, and then had risen again to lieutenant in 1869. Boutelle's experiences had left him a battle-hardened veteran cynical about civilian dabblers like Odeneal and Meacham. He was a man after William Tecumseh Sherman's own heart.

When the excited Applegate gave him his message, Boutelle was annoyed at having been disturbed. Boutelle told him to make himself comfortable, for he was going to have a long wait. Major John Green, the officer in charge of the fort, did not have enough troops to send into Modoc country.

"Uncle Johnnie," as his troops called Green, had worked up through the ranks, originally during the Mexican War. Breveted twice during the Civil War, he was now a major. Unquestionably brave, he had done well for himself, especially for someone who was a native-born German. (Years later he would retire, bitter after having been passed over for full colonel.)

Three hours later Boutelle was shocked when Green ordered him to make ready an excursion into the Lost River area. He could not have been pleased that he was going to be second in command on an operation that looked like a disaster in the making. Boutelle, moreover, was not someone to keep his opinions to himself.

Green had been swayed by Odeneal's opinion that only a show of force would be necessary. Odeneal's opinion, needless to say, Boutelle thought worse than worthless. But he dutifully prepared for the expedition. Having finished doing so by about 11:30, he then confronted Green. He reminded Green of General Canby's judgment that the Modocs would regard any such incursion by the American military as an act of war. He bluntly added that the thirty-eight men being sent would only be enough to start a fight, not to finish one.

Green admitted then that the white settlers were pressuring him against his best military judgment. "If I don't send the troops, they will think we are all afraid." Boutelle listened and buttoned his lip. To say what he thought might win him no more than a court-martial.

As the men rode out of Fort Klamath for the fifty-six-mile trek to Lost River, the weather fit Boutelle's mood: rain and sleet. The small force was commanded by Major James Jackson, another enlisted man commissioned during the Civil War who had made the army his career;

a few years later he would be awarded the Congressional Medal of Honor for action against the Nez Percé. Boutelle was uncomfortable at their orders, but easy under Jackson's command.

They arrived at Linkville, where they fed their horses, at supper time. Jackson met with Odeneal. Boutelle did not know, and never cared to ask, what transpired between them; but Applegate, who was now scout and translator for the expedition, seems to have been present at the interview. He later recorded Odeneal's instructions:

> When you arrive at the camp of the Modocs, request an interview with the head men and say to them that you did not come to fight or to harm them, but to have them go peaceably to Camp Yainax on Klamath Reservation, where ample provision has been made for their comfort and subsistence, and where, by treaty, they agreed to live. Talk kindly but firmly to them, and whatever else you may do, I desire to urge that if there is any fighting let the Indians be the aggressors. Fire no gun except in self-defense, after they have first fired upon you.

Waiting for an enemy to shoot you before defending yourself was a policy passing strange, but after supper the force immediately mounted and rode off. As tired as the men were, the decision was made, perhaps on Applegate's advice, that they leave the main trail because the Modocs would be likely to place lookouts along it. So the troops struggled through thick sagebrush in the dark. Daybreak found them a mile from Captain Jack's camp—in Boutelle's judgment, "a very tired lot of soldiers about to attempt a very disagreeable task."

Jackson, the experienced cavalry officer, ordered them to dismount and adjust their saddles. Boutelle apparently looked around and thought the group not fit for a battle. Although the rain had stopped, their jackets were largely wet through and in places frozen. Boutelle decided to buck up everyone's spirits.

Taking off his soaked overcoat, he declared that if he was going to fight he wanted to clear the decks for action, and he strapped the soggy coat to the cantle of his saddle. The men began to follow suit. Then they mounted and began to ride rapidly toward the Indian village, hoping to take the Modocs by surprise.

As they approached, they stumbled on a single Modoc, Bogus Charley, who was up early to do a little fishing in the river. Young and good looking, Bogus Charley was of all the Modocs the most fluent in

English. He could be completely charming when he wished, joking with Americans in their own rough-and-tumble frontier manner. He was named after a creek where he had once lived. But some Americans felt the name appropriate for other reasons. They never quite trusted a Modoc who moved so effortlessly between the white and Modoc worlds.

This brisk morning, Charley was not interested in charming the Americans. But before he could sprint to the camp to warn the Modocs, Jackson intercepted him.

"Where is Captain Jack?"

Charley answered slyly that the Modoc leader was still in his *wikiup*—but he didn't specify which one was Captain Jack's.

"I want to see him."

"What for?"

"I have an order for his arrest."

Bogus, pretending not to understand, now becoming defiant: "What do you want him for?"

Jackson, his patience fraying: "That makes no difference. Show me his tent."

Suddenly, the Americans were startled by the sharp report of a rifle.

The Modocs had divided themselves into two camps. The other was a mile or two away on the other side of the river. Scarfaced Charley was coming back across after a night of gambling. As he pulled his canoe ashore, he saw the American cavalry arrayed for an attack on the sleeping village, with Bogus Charley just standing there *talking* to the American commander.

As he clambered up the bank, Scarfaced Charley's rifle went off. He later claimed that he had accidentally discharged it when he stumbled in his excitement. Whether this was true or whether he was consciously trying to warn the Modocs, the village immediately came to life.

A general commotion ensued, as numerous Modocs looked out from their *wikiups* and saw the soldiers. The two platoons into which Jackson's force was divided dismounted and advanced at order arms in front of the horses. Applegate then entered the village and informed the few Modocs who would listen that he wanted to speak to Captain Jack. He assured them this was a friendly mission, but said Captain

Jack would have to go back to the reservation. He went from *wikiup* to *wikiup*, but could not find the Modoc leader.

At one point Applegate in frustration looked back toward Major Jackson (who was still mounted) and saw that Scarfaced Charley had finally reached the periphery of the village. The Indian was walking right past Jackson. The startled major ordered him to halt and pulled his pistol. Charley paid no attention, but continued toward the village, shouting. Gradually Applegate made out what Charley was saying, and it was not encouraging for a white man standing alone in the midst of Modocs. The Indian was telling the others to fight, fight to the death, don't hesitate, they could kill all the whites without losing a warrior. Scarfaced Charley, usually so reasonable, was in a fury.

But the Modocs were hesitating. In the Modoc village, people were running this way and that, calling to one another, snatching up children, leading the old people out of sight—nothing as yet belligerent. When Scarfaced Charley reached Applegate, he walked past the white man as if he did not exist. Charley was cursing as he entered a *wikiup*. The exasperated Jackson yelled after him, "You, chief, come here!"

Then came one of those moments that can be fixed in history like a painting.

The Modocs are still swirling around. Applegate still trying to talk. No one paying him the slightest mind. Jackson's men standing in front of their horses at order. Jackson still on his horse with his unfired pistol in his hand. Boutelle with all his attention focused on the *wikiup* into which Scarfaced Charley had just disappeared.

Suddenly Charley and one other warrior emerge from the *wikiup*, stripped to the buff, in war paint, a rifle in each hand. Charley is shouting once again, this time with his rifles in the air. Applegate can hear him yelling at the men to fight and telling the women and children to take cover. Those women and children near him fall flat to the ground as he ordered.

Applegate now turns to run back toward Jackson, yelling, "Major, they are going to fire!" Jackson cannot hear him, but the increasing commotion worries him. He rides quickly over to Boutelle.

"Mr. Boutelle, what do you think of the situation?" he asks with studied calmness.

Boutelle has no doubts. "There is going to be a fight, and the sooner you open it the better, before there are any more complete preparations."

Jackson seems to agree, but still tries to remain true to Odeneal's exhortation. He orders Boutelle to lead some men into the village and arrest Scarfaced Charley. This seems to Boutelle the height of stupidity, but he holds his tongue until Jackson has ridden off. As he put it later, "An attempt to arrest meant the killing of more men than could be spared if any of the survivors were to escape."

Boutelle calls to his dismounted men, "Shoot over those Indians."

At the same time he pulls his own pistol to shoot at Scarfaced Charley. One dead Modoc and the rest thoroughly scared, and maybe Jackson can achieve his objective with a minimum of fuss.

At precisely the same moment Charley decides that he had prepared his people enough for battle. He seeks out the most prominent target for the first American casualty, which happens to be Frazier Boutelle. They fire at one another simultaneously, and each comes within an inch of killing the other.

Charley's bullet tears through Boutelle's clothing at the elbow of his extended shooting arm. A slightly better shot, and the bullet would have gone through Boutelle's elbow and lodged in his chest. At the same instant the elbow is being taken out of Boutelle's shirt, the bandanna Charley had tied about his head is being perforated by Boutelle's bullet. A little better aim, and Charlie would have fallen with a bullet in the brain.

The firing is now general, but Boutelle's attention is still focused on Scarfaced Charley. As he shoots again at him, he sees Charley drop to the ground and crawl off into the sagebrush, whether wounded or not Boutelle cannot tell. Nor has he time to reflect because he sees another Indian, known as the Watchman, taking aim at him with a bow. As the arrow is released, Boutelle dives away and then shoots the archer. "The subsequent proceedings," Boutelle would write, "interested him no more."

Applegate in the meantime has to his amazement made it back to the troop unharmed, but his dazed impression of the battle is of chaos:

"Din and commotion; men falling in the line, the riderless horses dashing here and there and kicking among us."

Above it all he can hear the repeated shout from Major Jackson, "Fire! Fire! Fire!"

Eight of the Americans have already fallen. The Modoc warriors, shouting as one, now charge. Boutelle sees that his men are edging backward. His platoon is about to break. A retreat at this point means slaughter. He does the only thing he can. He yells "Forward!" and springs up, running directly at the main body of the Modocs, constantly firing. His men do likewise. The Modoc warriors now hesitate, and then retreat, yielding the village with the women, children, and old people.

Jackson has no desire to press his advantage. He can see the Modocs withdrawing in good order, prepared to punish any rash American advance. But Jackson and his men do not feel the slightest bit rash. Fully a third of Jackson's troops are down, dead or dying. The rest are completely exhausted.

Everyone realizes how close they have come to annihilation. Applegate puts it most simply: "Boutelle's calmness saved us."

The soldiers are convinced they have inflicted casualties on the Modocs equal to those they have suffered themselves. Those, for instance, who see Scarfaced Charley drop for cover as Boutelle shoots at him the second time are sure he has been killed. The Modocs, they are convinced, have been broken as a fighting force. The Modoc captives mournfully agree. Scarfaced Charley, Captain Jack, Curley Headed Doctor, Black Jim—the Americans are sure all are dead, although the only body they find is the Watchman's.

Satisfied, Jackson allows the women, children, and old folks to rejoin the men, and to take with them the Modoc horses. Applegate rails against this decision as "a mad piece of idiotic nonsense," but no one pays him any mind.

Green later wrote to his superiors, "The Indians or their leaders were determined on a fight at all hazards, and got enough of it, I think. The worst among them are undoubtedly killed, not less than sixteen of them being put out of the way."

Jackson had the village itself burned, inadvertently killing an old

woman who apparently had been left behind. It had been a costly battle, but they had won it. They were sure of that. Boutelle might bitterly reflect on "Mr. Odeneal, who would not trust his precious skin to a
council on Lost River, but preferred treacherously to send troops with
guns . . . believing that the Indians would not fight."

Nonetheless, even Boutelle, as he consoled his wounded men (some
dying slowly), did not yet see the significance of what had happened
that cold morning.

A war had just begun.

One who did understand was Odeneal. Soon after he learned about
the Battle of Lost River, he left Linkville heading north, hurrying to
put as much distance as possible between himself and the hostilities he
had done everything he could to start.

4

JACKSON'S TWO SQUADS of cavalry were not the only force to ride out of Linkville toward Lost River, nor the only one to do battle with Modocs.

Oliver Applegate, Ivan's brother, had been in Linkville when the troops passed through. He heard rumors that two Modocs from the Yainax reservation were spying on the movement of the troops, and he intended to ride to Lost River to warn Captain Jack of the impending attack. Deciding to head them off, Applegate, accompanied by an interpreter, rode quickly along the main trail to Lost River. A settler tagged along to see the fun, and as they traveled more and more joined up. By the time Applegate reached the Lost River region and set up his ambush his party numbered ten.

But it was the cavalry and not the Modoc spies, who passed by. Applegate shouted out from cover to his brother. Together, they decided that the civilian force should back up the army from the other side of the river. Oliver Applegate had apparently seen the second Modoc camp, up and across the river. It made sense for his men to cover this camp on the east side of the river while the army advanced on the other. As it turned out, the second camp included Hooker Jim and Curley Headed Doctor, persistent advocates of war against the whites. So Applegate and his men hurried across Natural Bridge and hid themselves in a gully a few hundred yards from Hooker Jim's camp, determined to be of use somehow.

When Scarfaced Charley's initial rifle shot was heard across the river, Oliver Applegate sent a man up the east bank to see what was happening. The scout came back breathlessly to inform Applegate that the Modocs were surrendering. That suited Oliver and the other men just fine. They emerged from their hiding place and began to ride nonchalantly toward Hooker Jim's still-sleeping camp. Bolstering their confidence, the first Modoc they met, another early riser, immediately gave up his weapon.

As they entered the camp, men were emerging from the *wikiups*, most still a little groggy. Curley Headed Doctor scowled at them, then offered Applegate a suspicious handshake. A moment later, Hooker Jim came out of his *wikiup*. He took one look at the American party, then started to slip quickly toward the canoes, trying not to draw attention to himself. He was seen, however, and cut off.

The warrior who had first given up his weapon now tried to grab it back. He was rebuffed, but Applegate suddenly began to realize that this was not going to be so simple. The Modocs themselves were starting to act as if they had little to fear from the badly outnumbered American band. The Americans were starting to realize that being surrounded in the open by a superior enemy was not an advantageous military position. With both sides momentarily frozen, perplexed, waiting for the other to make a move, there came from across the river the unmistakable sounds of battle.

Immediately all the Modoc warriors went for their weapons and started to shoot them wildly in the general direction of the Americans. The Americans lit out of the camp as fast as they could, firing back over their shoulders, not bothering to aim.

A Modoc woman with a baby panicked at the first shots and tried to mount an Indian pony, shouting, "No shoot! Me squaw! Me squaw!" It did no good. She and her baby were cut in two by a shotgun blast.

One American, having reached the edge of the camp, was horrified as his horse suddenly started to buck him off. Disoriented, the horse then bolted right back through the camp—and, reaching the river, wheeled around and ran back through it again, so wildly the Modocs never could get a good shot at the desperately clinging rider.

The Americans nearest Oliver Applegate during the retreat were appalled to hear him cackling the whole time, as if he were on a joy ride. On learning this later, Ivan Applegate vowed to "try to keep him out of any more fights" lest he end up "left in the sage brush."

Somehow the Americans managed to escape without any casualties. They would have, that is, had not three innocents wandered into Hooker Jim's camp later, completely ignorant of what had taken place. As they went to make the customary gestures of friendship, two were shot dead. The the third, badly wounded, managed to ride out and reach Applegate's men, who had holed up in a cabin nearby. He would never fully recover from his wound.

The Modocs, especially those of Hooker Jim's camp, were enraged at the unprovoked attacks. Apart from the Watchman, their warriors had received only minor injuries and wounds. But a number of women and children had been killed, three children in Hooker Jim's camp alone. The killing seemed to confirm all that Hooker Jim and Curley Headed Doctor had been saying about American treachery.

By the end of the day all the Modocs had gathered together far out of sight of the Americans, but still near the shore of Tule Lake. The decision was made to get all the women, children, and elderly out of harm's way. Captain Jack and most of the warriors of his camp took them across Tule Lake to the safety of the Lava Beds. The trip was dangerous at night, but the Modocs could not trust the Americans not to make another move against them in the morning.

Some of the men were in the small canoes favored by the Modocs, dugouts made from cedar trees found at the westernmost extent of the Modoc territory. These were only ten feet long and about two feet at the widest point—and could only carry two men at most. The women, children, and old people were crowded onto larger rafts, measuring ten by eight, which consisted of frameworks of three pine crosspieces, planked with a combination of juniper, willow, and bark, the whole tied together with tule rope or rawhide thongs. The rafts, as well as some of the canoes, were propelled by poling. So the Modocs, rather than directly crossing the lake, skirted its shore.

Scarfaced Charley did not join Captain Jack immediately in the Lava Beds; neither did Hooker Jim and his men.

Charley's action in helping precipitate the battle had been entirely out of character. He was frequently angry at the Americans, but only because they consistently did exactly the wrong thing. Whatever was most likely to undermine Captain Jack's authority and cause war, they were certain to do. They had done so this morning, but still Charley seemed to regret his own role.

He now rode on his own to warn friendly settlers that war had broken out. He told them to ride for their lives, and tell all they knew to do likewise. He seems to have been particularly concerned about the ranchers near Hot Creek who had long been friends of the Modocs. The only Modocs in Captain Jack's band not in the morning battle were those living at Hot Creek near the ranches of John Fairchild and Pressly Dorris. No American was more respected by the Modocs than Fairchild.

Fairchild had lived his whole life on the frontier. About thirty-eight years old but prematurely gray, with a long squared beard, he had been born in Mississippi when it was still largely wilderness. His family had apparently moved West during the Gold Rush. As a young man, he had been engaged in mining. The hit-or-miss of prospecting did not suit him, nor did the wild life of mining towns such as Yreka. He liked to think in the long term. He went into ranching and was successful. In the early 1860s he had moved his extensive herds to Hot Creek, well before the Modoc had signed away their lands in the treaty of 1864.

During the Civil War he had been outspoken in favor of Southern secession, so much so that a warrant was issued for his arrest. But no one, out of either respect or fear, saw fit to serve it. Fairchild did not like government and thought people should be left alone mostly. "People" in his way of thinking included the Modocs. Fairchild did not think much of the treaty whereby the Modocs gave up their lands. He respected their continuing claims and was willing to acknowledge their traditional title in whatever ways the Modocs thought appropriate. If that meant their taking the occasional cow for food, so be it.

As it happened, Pressly Dorris—Press, to his friends—was out looking for strays when Scarfaced Charley came upon him and warned him of what had happened. Dorris hurried back and told Fairchild. As Charley was behaving in character by trying to get settlers out of danger, so now Fairchild behaved in character. If he had been worried just about his own skin, he would have taken off south to Yreka. Instead, he worried about the Modocs living near him.

Those Modocs had nothing to do with the fight, yet they were now in great danger. He convinced them to let him and Dorris lead them to the Klamath reservation. That the Modocs agreed was a measure of their trust in Fairchild's judgment, for the Hot Creek warriors were as formidable as those of the other two camps.

The Hot Creek Modocs, although broadly professing allegiance to Captain Jack, were led by Shacknasty Jim (named for his mother's slovenly housekeeping). He was easily recognizable because he wore his hair long and parted in the middle; next to other Modoc men, he had an almost feminine look, which belied his reputation in battle.

The Hot Creek Modocs were notable for the young men who were prominent in their councils. Ellen's Man, for instance, moon-faced and so handsome he had been taken up by an influential older woman. Steamboat Frank, whose hefty mother puffed like a paddlewheel when she walked. Of the young Hot Creeks none was more impressive than Boston Charley, named for his light skin and fluency with English. Slenderly built, looking like little more than a boy, he was noted for his quick intelligence and easy manner. Along with Bogus Charley, he knew best how to beguile the Americans with humor, and enjoyed his own jokes so much he would sometimes fall down laughing.

These men were not afraid to fight; they, like Captain Jack, wanted peace if they could have it while retaining their freedom to work for men like Fairchild and Dorris. They agreed to allow the two ranchers to lead them toward the reservation. Unfortunately, they had to pass near Linkville on their way.

The trip to the outskirts of Linkville was uneventful. Fairchild and Press Dorris then told the Modoc families to make camp outside of town, while they themselves rode guard, lest any of the brave Linkville civilians decide to try something funny. When the bodies of those killed in the Battle of Lost River arrived in town, the sight, with a little help from alcohol, incited much of the town into a blood lust for vengeance. The Hot Creek Modocs were handy as suitable targets. A small party of eight or ten whites rode out of Linkville with the loudly expressed intent of hauling back a few Indians for lynching. Since the posse was well lubricated, its progress toward the Modoc camp was somewhat slow.

Fairchild and Dorris, warned of an impending expedition against them, intercepted the lynching party and managed to turn them back. Meanwhile, the Hot Creek Modocs were having second thoughts. If they must die at the hands of white men, they might as well die in battle, like men, rather than at the end of a rope. While Fairchild and Dorris were distracted elsewhere, the Hot Creeks slipped away with everything they could, including Fairchild's horse.

The route to the Klamath reservation was blocked, so they sought safety in the Lava Beds with Captain Jack.

If Scarfaced Charley stayed behind to work for peace after the battle of Lost River, Hooker Jim, Curley Headed Doctor, and other men of their camp did everything they could to assure war. They sent their families and elderly thirteen miles across Tule Lake with Captain Jack. They then made their own way to the Lava Beds by land, circling around the eastern shore of the lake where a number of settlers had established homesteads. Along the way, they sought out Henry Miller, supposedly their best friend among these settlers. The previous day they had asked him whether the military was about to move against them. He had said that as far as he knew they were not. As they now saw it, he had lied to allow the attack to catch them off guard. Pretending to be their friend, he obviously wanted them all dead.

Hooker Jim personally shot the unsuspecting Miller dead and mutilated his body. He and his men then rode from homestead to homestead, pillaging and killing all the men they could find. They were covered with blood when a white settler named Mrs. Shira first saw them. The white woman lived with her husband, Nicholas Shira, her father, William Boddy, her stepmother, and her father's two stepsons. The Boddy family were Australians who had come to California for the Gold Rush, but, unlike most of the newcomers from Down Under, they had decided to settle permanently.

Mrs. Shira sensed something amiss when a horse team returned alone from the field where the men were working. She ran the half-mile out to the field, only to find all her menfolk dead, every one shot through the head, as if executed. She returned to the house to tell her stepmother what had happened. Together, the two women began to flee toward the mountains that separated them from Linkville. They did not get far before they were intercepted by Hooker Jim and the rest.

One Modoc politely asked them if any men happened still to be in their house; the women assured them not. The Modocs then rode off with their stolen horses. Before they did, one Modoc said to the women, by way of explaining their grisly appearance but also to reassure them, "This is Boddy's blood. But we are Modoc. We do not kill women and children. You will find Boddy in the woods. We will not hurt you." The women could not have understood that he was contrasting the Modocs with the Americans who most assuredly did kill women and children, just as they had killed the women and children at Lost River.

Before Hooker Jim and his men were done, they had killed fourteen settlers, horribly butchering a few. One woman was able to save her twelve-year-old son by rushing toward the raiders while firing a Winchester; another saved both of her sons by barricading her house into a fort, using flour sacks as breastworks and drilling holes through the wall for firing loops. With so much easy prey around the lake, the raiding party had little taste for attacking mothers who showed this much pluck.

One woman widowed by the raid later wrote bitterly that the settlers had not been informed of the impending army action. "If these settlers had been warned in time not a white person would have been killed, as we all had arms and ammunition enough." Superintendent Odeneal did send out a warning party, but he did not think to order it to the eastern shore of Tule Lake, probably out of ignorance of the region.

Hooker Jim and his party, covered with blood and laden with plunder, arrived at Captain Jack's camp in the Lava Beds, apparently expecting to be welcomed as conquering heroes. Instead, Captain Jack denounced them. He wanted to surrender them to the white men. But now the Modocs who had recently arrived from Hot Creek made their voices heard. Hooker Jim had done to the settlers only what the settlers had intended to do to their band, which had shed no blood. The Linkville lynchers had convinced the Hot Creek band that war was inevitable.

The meeting was long and contentious. In the end Captain Jack confronted the choice of leading all the Modocs in war against the whites or of losing his standing as a headman. The Hot Creek Modocs may have tipped the balance against him. Curley Headed Doctor also told the debating warriors that he had rituals that would assure not only their final victory, but also the complete disappearance of the white man and the happy return of all the Modoc dead.

The Modocs knew about the realm of the spirits where the dead lived, and they feared it. The dead could appear to the living at night and talk

to them, usually in dreams. It was dangerous to have a dream of someone newly dead—it was as if a dead person for a brief time had power
to entice your spirit to leave your body.

However, a spirit could leave its body and then return. A powerful
shaman could on rare occasions raise someone from the dead by induc-
ing his own soul to leave his body and find the soul of the recently dead
along the flowery path to the spirit realm and lead it back.

This the Modocs believed, as did the Klamaths and the Paiutes.
Then the Paiute seer Wovoka went all the way to the spirit realm and
came back with a great revelation. He said he had gone into the mountains to cut wood and heard a noise above him on the mountain. He laid
down his ax and started in the direction of the noise, just out of curios-
ity. Then suddenly he fell down dead and was taken straightaway to
the spirit realm.

What he learned there was wonderful. The Indian race was going to
inherit the earth, an earth restored to its pristine state. All the Indians
who ever lived were coming back, to live on this renewed earth without death, disease, hunger, or pain. Life would be eternal, happiness
perfect. The white man would simply disappear, spontaneously com-
bust, leaving not even ashes behind.

The living could assist the Indian dead to return by dancing the
Ghost Dance. In late 1870 or early 1871, the dance spread from Nevada,
where Wovoka still lived, to the Paiute Snakes of Yainax Reservation,
and from them to the Klamaths and Modocs. Curley Headed Doctor
was a Ghost Dance convert, and he led the Modocs of Captain Jack's
band in the new ritual.

A rope of twisted tule was laid to encircle the dance ground. A pole
was raised in the center and hung with various objects of power. A
bough of sagebrush was used to sprinkle water on those about to
dance. Lines of red and black were drawn on their whitened faces, ver-
tical on men, horizontal on women. The dancers formed a circle around
the pole, holding hands. Then the dance began.

Step with one foot, drag the other behind; step with one foot, drag
the other behind; again and again and again. Always to the left. All the
while repeating over and over a simple chant.

The chants the Modocs used have not survived; but the Paiutes' chants, presumably much the same, have. All of them point in simple images toward an apocalyptic violence:

> The black rock, the black rock,
> The black rock, the black rock,
> The rock is broken, the rock is broken,
> The rock is broken, the rock is broken.

Or:

> There is dust from the whirlwind,
> There is dust from the whirlwind,
> There is dust from the whirlwind,
> The whirlwind on the mountain,
> The whirlwind on the mountain,
> The whirlwind on the mountain.

Or:

> Fog! Fog!
> Lightning! Lightning!
> Whirlwind! Whirlwind!

For hours and hours the dancers shuffled, the step never varying, the chant the same, over and over again, around the pole, within the tule rope circle.

Anyone who stopped or interrupted the dance by stepping into the charmed circle would immediately be turned into rock, black rock that would be broken into dust, dust to be blown away by the whirlwind of the end of time. It was a dance of fog, lightning, whirlwind, and the restoration of the earth in its perfect fullness to its chosen people.

Finally a few dancers began to drop, and those now stepping over and around them to keep dancing knew the spirits of the fallen had left their bodies. They also knew that when these chosen ones revived they would tell what the coming-back people wished done.

When the morning came and the sun rose again, the dance ended. The dancers threw themselves into the nearest water, whether river or lake. They made the plunge even in deep winter, so cold that they emerged with ice in their hair.

No one knew exactly when the dead would come back, only that it would be soon. They would come from the east, at the time of year when the new grass was about eight inches high.

The dead were coming back, that was sure. So Curley Headed Doctor told the Modocs they need not mourn the dead, nor fear death themselves. Nor need the Modocs fear the white men who, numerous though they might be, were doomed and knew it not.

When news of the Tule Lake massacre reached the broader world, influential western voices declared it to be the fault of the peace policy. *The Overland Monthly* of San Francisco denounced the peace party as "reservation people," while conveniently forgetting that only men were killed:

> The pity of it is—the grievous pity—that it was the settlers who were bitten and not the reservation people. . . . The blood of those poor women and children lies not more upon the bloody-minded Modocs than it does upon the wretched, slabbering, paltering policy which let them loose. What the Modocs need more than anything else is that tremendous thrashing which one brave man gives another and which they can understand. After that, impartial justice—no swindling, no fooling, no generosity!

"Uncle Johnnie" Green, now realizing that the Modocs were far from broken as a fighting force, hoped that Fairchild and Dorris could intervene to help avoid a war. He wanted the ranchers to assure the Modocs that "if those men who committed the murders after the fight are surrendered, they will all be received and protected. What occurred during the fight I consider warfare and they will not be held responsible. . . . I wish you would inform Capt. Jack that he need expect no mercy if he does not surrender now, as there are troops on their way to his country, and more coming."

California newspapermen began to arrive in Linkville to cover the Modoc trouble. One from the *San Francisco Evening Bulletin* described Linkville as a town of "fifty inhabitants, two stores, a hotel, blacksmith shop and the requisite number of whisky shops." This little village, he thought, had been doing well because "it has the trade of the settlers for miles around." Now, with a war nearby, it was going to do even better.

Newspapermen found much good copy in the arguments and conversations overheard in the Linkville hotel and saloons, as two hundred reinforcements under the command of Colonel Frank Wheaton arrived for the campaign against the Modocs. Some residents were sanguine about the war; others far less so.

"That's enough to eat up Jack's little band. Keep cool, my dear friends. Let 'em go for 'em. They need a lickin' bad. There won't be a grease spot left of 'em."

"Look-er here, stranger, I'll bet you a hundred head of cows that Captain Jack whips them there two hundred soldiers like hell. So I will. I know what I'm talking about, I do. I tried them Modoc fellows long time ago. They won't lick worth a damn, no they won't. If Frank Wheaton goes down there a puttin' on style like a big dog in tall rye, he'll catch hell. So he will. I'm going down just to see the fun."

"You're a crazy old fool. Frank Wheaton with two hundred soldiers will wipe 'em out 'fore breakfast."

"Look-er here if I'm crazy the cows ain't. Come, come, if you think I'm crazy, come, up with the squivalents, and you can go into the stock-raisin' business cheap. You can."

Getting no takers on his proffered wager, the crazy old man with cows now began to explain why he was so certain:

Major Jackson went down there t'other day with forty men, and Jack hadn't fourteen bucks with him, and he licked Jackson out of his boots in no time, and that was in open ground, and Jackson had the drap on the Injuns at that. And by thunder he got the worst lickin' a man ever got in this neck of the woods. So he did. Then another thing. Captain Jack ain't in open ground now. Not in a damned sight. He is in the all-firedest place in the world. You've been to the Devil's Garden at the head of Sprague River, haven't you? Well, that place ain't a patchen to that ere place where the Injuns is now. I've been there, and I tell you it's nearly lightenin', all rocks and caves, and you can't lead a horse through it in a week. And them the Injuns knows every inch of the ground, and when they get in them there caves, why it tain't no use talking, I tell you, you can't kill nary an Injun. You can't! I'm going down just to see the fun.

The two hundred men under the direct command of Colonel Frank Wheaton were only half the force being sent against Captain Jack. Another two hundred were coming under the command of Captain R. F. Bernard and Colonel E. C. Mason.

Many of the soldiers were soon congregated near Fairchild's ranch. The whole force now numbered four hundred, the regular army troops reinforced by companies of volunteers from Oregon and California. The California volunteers were mostly men who worked for Fairchild and Dorris. The Oregon volunteers came from places such as Linkville and its environs; they, in particular, spoiled for a fight. Perhaps more than a few of them had been in the lynching party sent out to get the Hot Creek Modocs.

At one point the Oregon volunteers became impatient at the training exercises they were being put through. Having noticed a few women and children from the Hot Creek band who had returned to Fairchild's ranch, they proposed to practice war on them.

"Nits make lice. Let's take them boys. Here goes."

But before they could act Fairchild interposed himself: "No, you don't. Not yet. Take me first. No man harms defenseless women where I am, while I am standing on my perpendiculars."

"Who are you?"

"Try me, and you will find out that I am John Fairchild. Who are your officers?"

Fairchild, having temporarily intimidated the men, then sought out their officers and blistered them. Fairchild was not a man to mince his words. His words on this occasion have been left unrecorded. A reporter who overheard them said they were neither classical nor biblical but effective nonetheless. He could not print them, for if he omitted the profanities there would be little left.

The military plan was to approach Captain Jack's stronghold simultaneously from the west and the east. One half of the force bivouacked near Hooker Jim's old camp, and then skirted around the eastern shore of Tule Lake, following exactly the route of the escaping marauders. They meant to take up positions between the Lava Beds and Clear Lake, where the Applegates had their ranch.

The other half of the force, Fairchild with it, came from Hot Creek and approached the Lava Beds from the west. Their camp was only about two miles from the beginning of the Lava Beds, but a full thirteen from Captain Jack's stronghold, which was now effectively cut off from the outside world. The Americans were in no hurry. Troops and armaments gradually arrived throughout December. Linkville merchants began to follow the time-honored western practice of gouging the army sent to save them; prices for saddles and the like quickly doubled. War meant good business.

The Van Bremer brothers, whose ranch was even closer to the troops, charged prices that made even Linkville's look reasonable. The soldiers came cordially to detest these brothers who returned the favor while raking in their war profits.

Soldiers and others curious about the infamous Lava Beds could get an overview by climbing a high bluff to the west. The first glance was misleading. One newspaperman, when the Beds were pointed out, thought there must be some mistake. He said in disappointment, "Where are the Lava Beds? This country below looms like a flat plain that a mounted man could gallop across without difficulty or impediment."

From the bluff the Lava Beds presented a surface apparently as smooth as that of Tule Lake itself. The Beds from this height took on a gray hue, the dullness contrasting on a sunny day with the sheen of the lake. Here and there in the Beds were dark spots, almost pure black, some of them long and narrow, others rounded or oval, others jagged and irregular. These were the caves and ravines in the lava, although from that distance they looked like no more than shadows from clouds. They were, nonetheless, visual hints that what appeared to be a regular surface was really a chaos of rock.

The American squads sent out to reconnoiter the Lava Beds got a closer look, the first sight most of the troops had ever had of such a formation. It was, as one report put it, "one hell of a place." Riding through the lava beds was like traveling a vast sea petrified during a storm. They were comprised of a series of swells hundreds of feet long (running roughly north to south) and twenty feet high, with smaller waves, and even foam, of solid rock.

Some soldiers of literary inclination attempted to capture the landscape in words. One wrote that the Lava Beds were a black ocean tumbled into a thousand fantastic shapes, a wild chaos of ruin, desolation and barrenness—a wilderness of billowy upheavals, of furious whirlpools, of miniature mountains rent asunder, of gnarled and knotted, wrinkled and twisted masses of blackness, and all this far-stretching waste of blackness with its thrilling suggestiveness of life, of action, of boiling, surging, furious motion was petrified—all stricken dead and cold in the instant of its maddest rioting—fettered, paralyzed and left to glower at heaven in impotent rage for evermore.

This rage did not seem impotent to those Americans who had to travel across the Lava Beds by foot. The men had to clamber up and down continually, with the lava tearing at their boots and clothes, their fingers soon raw, every handhold wearing away a little skin. It was as if the rocky-foam of the lava surface was really comprised of millions of parasites, each mindlessly seeking its own little drop of blood.

The broad regularity of these lava swells quickly came to seem like a rocky mirage. Once within the Beds, the soldier saw only the limitless variety, each new lava formation seeming to have its own trick for making a man take a tumble. The only way to remain oriented was to take your bearing by the lake. Unless, of course, you were a Modoc. Then every twist and turn in the rocks had a name, a history, even a myth.

If Lost River was God's Smile for the Modocs, the Lava Beds were His Grimace. The Modocs called the place "the land of burnt-out fires." One of the Applegates agreed; he described it as "hell with the fires gone out," and added that it would turn into hell with the fires relit for any American force that tried to dislodge the Modocs:

> An Indian can fire from the top of one of these stone pyramids, shoot a man without exposing an inch of himself. He can, without haste, load and shoot a common muzzle-loading rifle ten times before a man can scramble over the rocks and chasms between slayer and slain. If at this terrible expense of life, a force dislodges him from his cover, he has only to drop into and follow some subterraneous passage with which he is familiar to gain another ambush, from which it will cost ten more lives to dislodge him.

Only a few patrols sent out on reconnaissance encountered Modocs. One small party, having done its survey without raising any sign of an Indian, noticed a stunning white horse wandering around the Beds just beyond the limits they had been ordered to go. A few soldiers started after it, then thought better. When they stopped, a disappointed shout came from the Beds. "Come on! Come on!"

Others in a supply train attacked by a Modoc raiding party were less fortunate. One driver was killed outright and the guard driven off. Private Sidney Smith was later found stripped, scalpless, and earless, with bullet wounds in his leg, head, stomach. He was still alive, but not for long.

Colonel Wheaton did not reach the front until late December. He and Canby agreed that the longer they could wait, the weaker the Modocs would be when they went in after them. Canby wrote to his superiors, "I do not think the operations will be protracted. The snow will drive the Indians out of the mountains and they cannot move without leaving trails that can be followed. It will involve some hardships upon the troops; but they are better provided and can endure it better than the Indians. In that respect, the season is in our favor."

Wheaton concurred: "We will be prepared to make short work of the impudent and enterprising savages."

However, with profiteers like the Van Bremers sucking their blood, not all the troops thought the waiting and the hardships worth it. One of them later wrote bitterly, "And for what? To drive a couple of hundred miserable aborigines from a desolate natural shelter in the wilderness, that a few thriving cattlemen might ranch their wild steers in a scope of isolated country, the dimensions of some several reasonable sized counties."

What the American did not know was that the Modocs had found Pressly Dorris's strays, about a hundred head, grazing peacefully on grass outcroppings within the Lava Beds themselves. Thus they were better supplied with meat than the soldiers who had to depend on the kind ministrations of the brothers Van Bremer.

On January 15, 1873, Wheaton wrote to Canby that his howitzers had arrived and that the men firing them had been adequately drilled. All was ready.

"We leave for Capt. Jack's Gibraltar tomorrow morning and a more enthusiastic, jolly set of Regulars and volunteers I never had the pleasure to command. If the Modocs will only try to make good their boast to whip a thousand soldiers, all will be satisfied. . . . I don't understand how they can think of any serious resistance tho' of course we are prepared for their fight or flight."

That same night, around a camp fire, the Oregon volunteers treat John Fairchild to their enthusiastic jollity.

A captain of the volunteers half-jokingly frets, "I have but one fear, and that is I can't restrain my men. They are so eager to get at 'em. They will eat the Modocs up raw, if I let 'em go."

Fairchild responds, "Don't fret, you can hold them. They won't be hard to keep back when the Modocs open fire."

The men, however, have taken to cannibalistic blustering.

"I say, Jim, are you going to carry grub?"

"No, I am going to take Modoc sirloin for my dinner."

Another pipes in, "I think that I'll take mine rare."

Yet another, who has probably heard tales from Yreka, explains that he will be looking for a comely squaw to . . . do his washing. Another says he intends to ride back to California on Captain Jack's horse, by which he seems to mean the white one that was bait for a possible ambush.

The conviviality in the American camps contrasts with the grimness in Captain Jack's. Link River Jack, always devious, has snuck through the lines. He tells the Modocs of the outrage among the Americans at the slaughter of the settlers. He tells them of the large army that is poised to strike against them any moment. Maybe he just enjoys bringing the dire news. Yet, at least according to one account, he holds out hope for the Modocs. If they can repulse the Americans for a little while, he is sure that the Klamaths and the Snakes will enter on their side.

If Link River Jack did give the Modoc this assurance, then his mission was malicious mischief. Half the Oregon volunteer force is made up of Klamath warriors, enlisted as scouts under the leadership of Oliver Applegate. They are camped within a day's march of the stronghold. They are wearing white badges in their hair, lest some overzealous American mistakenly go after a Klamath sirloin for his dinner.

The Modocs now have to decide between giving up Hooker Jim, Curley Headed Doctor, and the others, or doing battle against the Americans.

Jack pleads with his people, using arguments he has heard from Old Schonchin:

> We have made a mistake. We cannot stand against the white men. Suppose we kill all these soldiers. More will come, and still more, and finally all the Modocs will be killed. When we kill the soldiers, others will take their places. But when a Modoc gets killed, no man will come to take his place. We must make the best terms we can. I do not want to fight the white man. I want no war. I want peace. Some of the white men are our friends. They told us not to fight the white men. We want no war. Soon all the young men will be killed. We do not want to fight.

Schonchin John, Jack's bellicose rival as head of the band, argues that war is the only choice. He reminds them, as usual, of the Ben Wright massacre. Then he argues that all white men are so many Ben Wrights: "We have nothing to expect from the white men. We can die, but we will not die first. I won't give up. I want to fight. I can't live long. I am an old man."

Scarfaced Charley does his best to support Captain Jack: "I was mad on Lost River. My blood was bad. I was insulted. I have many friends among the white men. I do not want to kill them. We cannot stand against the white men. True, I am a Modoc. What their hearts are, my heart is. Maybe we can stop this war. I want to live in peace."

Finally, Curley Headed Doctor puts his religious authority fully behind the war: "My hands are red with the white man's blood. I was mad when I saw the dead women and children on Lost River. I want war. I am not tired. The white men cannot fight. They shoot in the air. I will make medicine that will turn the white man's bullets away from the Modocs. We will not give up. We can kill all that come."

The vote is thirty-seven to fourteen in favor of war. Captain Jack's response is simple. "This is the last of my people. I must do what their hearts say. I am a Modoc, and I am not afraid to die." Without complaint, he turns to make preparation for battle. He is particularly worried about having enough ammunition. He asks Queen Mary to make bullets from the metal of guns too old to fire.

Curley Headed Doctor has a red rope of braided tule laid out, encircling the stronghold. No Modoc will be touched by white bullets, and no white man will set foot within the red circle. On that double promise Curley Headed Doctor is pledging his life.

During that night they dance the Ghost Dance, and Curley Headed Doctor in a trance walks the flowery path to the spirit realm.

The Americans intend to march into the Lava Beds simultaneously from east and west. They will deploy in half circles. When their southern wings join, they will have Captain Jack's stronghold boxed against the shore of Tule Lake.

The soldiers and volunteers to the west of the Modoc are awakened at 4 A.M. on January 17, 1873, to prepare for the attack. They rise in the cold dark, grumbling at the chill wind blowing off the lake. A thick fog does not help spirits. Breakfast is coffee and hard tack. Then they are ordered to fall in. Roll is called, each man answering "Here!" to his name. Then comes the call "Forward on the line."

Thus they begin their march into the Lava Beds. They are amazed at the fog. One officer who watches the advance from a bluff nearby cannot see the Lava Beds at all and quickly loses sight of the men.

"As I stood on the bluff and gazed out above the lava-bed that morning, it conveyed the impression of an immense lake. A mist or fog hung over it, so dense that nothing transpiring therein was visible, while about us at the top of the bluff all was clear. To see the column go half way down and then disappear from view entirely was, to say the least, uncanny and might have suggested the words of Dante's 'Inferno,' 'All hope abandon, ye who enter here.'"

The fog gives the Americans cover as they advance, but the lack of visibility also makes the howitzers useless.

Fairchild, Dorris, and their California volunteers are on the left wing, nearest to the lake. With the dawn the fog is starting to thin slightly. The grotesque shapes of the lava in the fog look weird, threatening. Sound seems to travel well across the Lava Beds in the cold of this morning, as if the fog enhances hearing as it impairs sight. Firing is heard on the right, and from a mile away the guns snap crisply like bunches of firecrackers. It is the brave Oregonians, on the right wing, shooting at shadows.

The progress is slow but adequate given the rough terrain. The officers regularly give encouragement to the men. "Steady, boys. Steady."

Fairchild adds his own. "Go slow, boys, go slow. You'll raise 'em directly." But they don't. The tension and the cold make it seem that they have traveled much farther than they have.

One of Fairchild's men says, perhaps with more relief in his voice than he intends, "Just as I expected. They've left. I knew they wouldn't stand and fight when the volunteers got after them."

Another concurs, "They knew we was comin'."

But Fairchild intervenes. "Steady there. We'll raise them pretty soon. They hain't run. They're thar for sure. Go slow, boys. Keep down, boys. Keep down low, boys."

Through the fog they hear a rumbling ahead of them that is later described as like a train crossing a great bridge. The men immediately realize that this means the eastern force has made contact, or is it the howitzers?

Exultation goes through the men.

"Bernard's opened on 'em. Now we will go. Hurrah! We'll take 'em in the rear. Hurrah! Hurrah! Hurrah for hell!"

In the still lingering fog it's hard to tell if this is one man or a number singing out. But one regular cannot help making a joke at the last cheer.

"That's right. Every man hurrah for the country he's going to."

Flashes are seen from the direction where the Modocs are supposed to be, flashes in the fog with the crisp sound of muskets. Suddenly Roberts, Fairchild's second in command, is down, blood spurting from his neck, drenching the rocks nearby that are already damp from the fog. Another man goes down, as quietly and limp as Roberts.

Major Green shouts "Fire!" The bugle confirms the order. The other officers echo. The men obey. No one has seen a Modoc. Men still crumple right and left.

One of Fairchild's men is yelling, "Damn your souls! Get me out of here! Can't you see I'm shot? My thigh is broke."

The men by now have oriented themselves to where the Modoc fire seems to be coming from, the flashes of their muskets apparently giving away their position. For hour after hour they make slow progress, fired on by an enemy they cannot see, firing back in the general direction of the phantoms. Indians are everywhere yet nowhere.

One private crawls over the crest of a lava swell, careful not to expose himself—only to be mortally wounded in the stomach, from below. He has passed over a crevice with a Modoc in it.

A young volunteer near him reflects later on what he learned that morning: "Bravery is only pride and good control over your legs." He adds by way of afterthought that his own "legs wanted to run but pride held them in check."

The line of advance is becoming ragged. Wheaton looks for the Oregon volunteers and does not find them. They're back a piece, he is told, under a nice lava ledge, in safety. Wheaton sends a scout to order them up to the front. For some reason they don't get the message—or, having got it, don't understand it. After taking a few casualties early, they prefer to listen to the battle from a distance.

The nineteen Klamath scouts, among them Link River Jack, are even more timid than the Oregon volunteers. As one officer puts it in disgust, they "only fired their rifles in the air and did some tall talking, but did not do any service as far as I have been able to ascertain." The Modocs taunt them, telling them to leave their ammunition behind when they retreat. The Americans half-believe that the spooked Klamaths will cut and run.

Fairchild's volunteers are approaching the stronghold, near where they might link up with the wing of the eastern force on the shore of Tule Lake. The fog has lifted, or rather retreated back across the lake. It is unfortunate timing for the Californians because these last hundred yards offer little cover, a circumstance the Modocs have not failed to notice. The volunteers are soon pinned down by Modoc fire. Three more are hit. Then Fairchild and Dorris hear a familiar Indian voice— Steamboat Frank is calling to Scarfaced Charley.

"Hello! Charley, here is some Yreka boys. Don't you see them?"

Charley shouts back in his distinctive basso, "Yes."

Steamboat continues, ending each question now with a rifle shot.

"Boys, what do you want? [Shot.] What makes you come here to fight us? [Shot.] Charley, there is old Dorris! [Shot.] Say, Dorris, how long are you going to fight us? [Shot.] What's the matter with you Dorris? [Shot.] Can't you hear? [Shot.] Ain't you got ears? [Shot.] Can't you talk? [Shot.] Ain't you got a mouth? [Shot.]"

Dorris knew the best way to keep ears (and scalp) was to keep his own counsel for the time being.

The Yreka boys are not the only ones being taunted. Captain David Perry has a man fall near him. He imprudently exposes himself, looking up to see how badly he is hit, only to be hit himself through the arm. He yells with pain, immediately to be greeted by Modoc jeers, including what sounds like the voice of a woman: "You come here to fight Indians and you make a noise like that. You no man, you squaw."

The sunlight now glares off the lava, making it sparkle in places but failing to warm the air. Despite the glare, the regulars to Fairchild's right can see what is happening to his men, with the lack of cover and the withering fire. But they can't see the Modocs responsible for the shooting, and they have only the most general sense of where those Modocs are under cover. They have to trust their ears, as their eyes do no good. These regulars are refusing to advance any further.

Major Green, realizing what is happening, rushes to them. Then to everyone's amazement he jumps up on a podium of lava, fully exposing himself to Indian fire, and delivers an exhortation. One version has him shouting only, "Forward my men. Up the cliff. Come my men. Up! up!" Yet hardened cursers later will remember being as impressed by the inventiveness of his oaths as they are by his bravery. Green will win the Congressional Medal of Honor for his actions, if not his words. But right now all his heroic urging on of his men accomplishes is to increase the growing mound of blue-clad bodies.

It is now late afternoon. The western force has made it to within fifty yards of the stronghold. Fairchild is close enough that only an arm of Lake Tule separates him from Bernard's forces. Bernard yells across the lake to report that he has more wounded men than he can take care of.

When Wheaton hears this from a messenger, he is stunned. He knows and respects Bernard. Bernard has been so badly mauled that his men are in no condition to attempt a final assault. That's the real message.

Wheaton absently asks an experienced Indian fighter standing near him, "What had we better do?"

"Get the hell out of here, by God," is the answer.

Wheaton orders that all units take cover until dark and then withdraw.

Dusk. Tule Lake sends a frigid tide of fog back to envelop the Lava

Beds. This is a mercy, for the little army in its retreat is near panic. Prostrate wounded see the withdrawal starting and plead not to be left behind. Some have to be. They are too close to the Modocs. Rescue attempts produce only more wounded men. One of the wounded calls out to be shot. "Don't leave me alive for the Modocs."

Between the fog and the dark, the soldiers can scarcely make out objects a foot away. As one puts it, "We had to feel rather than see our way." The jagged lava does its worst on what is left of boots, uniforms, bodies, spirits. The forces are all jumbled together now, no order at all. As one of the men recalls later, "Our position was critical in the extreme. One shot would have precipitated a stampede." But no shot comes. The exhausted men stumble back into their camp at about 2 A.M.

At dawn the victorious Modocs plunder the battlefield. They are now well stocked with repeating rifles and ammunition, and with plenty of clothes for the winter.

Queen Mary and the women come out to do the scavenging, and to finish off the wounded. The women find two soldiers still alive and stone them to death before stripping and scalping them. Schonchin John's teenage son, Peter, is with the women; running across the lava, his arms filled with booty, he slips and a pistol goes off, maiming his hand. He's the most serious Modoc casualty in what comes to be called the First Battle for the Stronghold.

The American army of four hundred, by contrast, has lost thirty-seven men—twelve dead or dying of their wounds, twenty-five seriously wounded. Fifty-three Modoc warriors have inflicted this defeat.

Curley Headed Doctor is exultant: "I promised you a medicine that would turn the white man's bullets. Where is the Modoc that has been struck with the white man's bullets? I told you the Great Spirit was on our side. Your chief's heart was weak. Mine was strong. We can kill all the white men that come."

Schonchin John publicly congratulates the shaman on his power: "I felt strong when I saw the fog that our medicine man had brought over the rocks yesterday morning. I knew we could kill the soldiers. We are Modocs."

Shacknasty Jim and the Hot Creek Modocs share in the celebration. Shacknasty Jim boasts, "I can stand off twenty of them volunteers now because I have got me a nice Henry rifle and plenty of cartridges. I also have plenty of volunteer hats."

Captain Jack, however, holds his ground. Despite the victory he is still advocating peace:

> It is true we have killed many white men. The Modoc heart is strong. The Modoc guns were sure. The bullets went straight. We are all here. But hear me, my people. The white men are many. They will not give up. They will come again. More will come next time. No matter how many the Modocs kill, more will come each time, and we will all be killed after a while. I am your voice. My blood is Modoc. I will not make peace until the Modoc heart says "Peace." We will not go on the warpath again. Maybe this war will stop.

Again the Modocs dance, this time with fresh scalps on their sacred pole.

Back in the American camp, Fairchild overheard the Oregon volunteers making excuses for themselves. The defeat was the fault of the regular army.

"It takes volunteers to fight Injuns. Rather have one hundred volunteers anytime than a regiment of regulars."

"I tell you ain't them Modocs nearly thunder though? But the regulars fire from the hip. They could not get down and draw a fine bead."

"The captain says he's going to raise a new company, picked men. And then the Modoc will get hell. Won't they though?"

Fairchild had heard enough. He treated the men to a specialty of his, sarcasm as galling in its way as Modoc fire.

"How did you like your Modoc sirloin, eh? Putty good, eh? Didn't take it raw, did you? Where's that fellow who was going to bring home a good-looking squaw for a . . . dishwasher? Wonder how he likes her about this time? Where's that other fellow who was going to ride Captain Jack's pacing horse?"

Letting it sink in that those two were dead (they were killed early in the fighting), he then added cruelly, "Wonder if those boys who were spoiling for a fight are out of danger?"

Fairchild, now in a cold rage, recognized volunteers who had wanted to kill the Hot Creek Modoc living near his ranch, just for practice. "Say, boys, there's some old squaws over there near the spring. They ain't got any guns. Ain't no bucks there. Maybe you can take them."

Fairchild cocked his head to one side, a habit of his when angry. He sought out the gaze of the captain who had worried about holding his boys back. Then asked sarcastically where they had been during the fight. He concluded his diatribe with what amounted to a summation:

> Now, Captain, let me give you a bit of advice. It won't cost you nothing. When you raise another company to fight the Modocs, don't you take any of them fellows that you can't hold back. Nor them fellows who want to eat Modoc steaks raw. They ain't a good kind to have when you get in a tight place. Why, Shacknasty Jim could whip four of them at a time. Them fellows ain't worth a continental damn for fighting Modocs. Better leave them fellers with their mammies.

A little later, calmly reflecting on the battle, Fairchild wrote a friend, "I have been a good many close places but that beat anything."

He still could not believe the heroics of Green: "Major Green took more chances than any man I ever saw. He walked the lines and gave his orders during the hottest of the fight and never took shelter or dodged. It looked like a miracle he escaped."

At his breakfast of hard tack and coffee the morning after the battle, Colonel Wheaton was ashen.

He said to no one in particular, "I have seen something of war, something of fortifications." He added, "I do not believe a hundred thousand men in a hundred thousand years could construct such fortifications."

Such exaggerations were not like him, but he knew he would have the unpleasant task that day of writing to explain to Canby what had gone wrong. Now, at least, he had a realistic sense of the task ahead, as his letter indicates:

> We fought the Indians through the lava-beds to their stronghold, which is in the center of miles of rocky fissures, caves, crevices, gorges and ravines, some of them one hundred feet deep. In the opinion of many experienced officers, regulars or volunteers, one thousand men would be required to dislodge them from their almost impregnable position, and it must be deliberately with a free use of mortar batteries. The Modocs were scarcely exposed at all to our persistent attacks. They left one

ledge to gain another equally secure. . . . No troops could have fought
better than all did, in the attack advancing promptly and cheerfully
against an unseen enemy over the roughest rock country imaginable.

Wheaton had to admit to Canby, however, that all he had achieved
was "a forced reconnaissance." Canby held Wheaton responsible, and
began immediately to make plans to replace him.

Bernard in the eastern camp was planning to write his own report.
He was perhaps the most unlikely commander to serve in the Modoc
War. He had grown up in the border country of Tennessee and had
joined the Union army as a private, to work as a blacksmith. By the
end of the war he was a captain, having been breveted twice for bravery. Since the Civil War he had been cited once again, this time for action against the Apaches. In short, R. F. Bernard was not someone
squeamish about war and its horrors.

Still, Bernard used his report as an occasion to express his outrage
at having to fight the Modocs. While Wheaton and others were writing
about the Modocs in military terms, Bernard, the ex-blacksmith, decided to discuss the whole situation in moral terms.

"These Indians have acted more humanely, in every instance, than
we have. The only thing they claim or ask is a home at the mouth of the
Lost River, where they were born and raised. . . . They have fought like
men fighting for their rights, and if any man should have, or could gain
their rights by fighting for them, the Modocs are more than entitled to
what they claim."

Bernard did not think that after this battle the American troops
were in any condition to fight. The men were "so badly demoralized
that they could hear the whizzing of balls, and the war-hoops of Indians
for the next twenty-four hours; besides, two thirds of the command
was so badly bruised and used up that they are limping about yet." He
added for the sake of emphasis, "Many of the troops that have seen the
place would rather serve twenty years on Alcatraz for desertion than
attack the enemy again in the lava beds." Bernard, however, wanted to
emphasize matters broader than military. "It seems cruel that human
life should be sacrificed in such a manner for the gratification of a few
unscrupulous dollar hunters."

He concluded forcefully: "This tribe was living in peace, subsisting
themselves without the aid of anyone, when the attempt was made to

force them to leave their native place, and to go and live amongst a people that have always been their bitterest enemies and who are now employed in the field against them. Men that would not fight under such circumstances are not worthy of life or liberty."

Back at the western camp, the Van Bremer brothers were still finding new ways to exploit the troops. Rains had come, and the roads to Linkville were all but impassable. Supply trains covered as little as two miles a day in the mud. When the supply wagons failed to arrive and eggs were needed for the wounded, the Van Bremers supplied six, at fifty cents apiece. They refused to be paid in army script. One officer had to pay for the eggs out of his own pocket. Later he wrote, "From that time until our departure I spent a considerable portion of my time in studying human villainy with the Van Bremers as a model."

The Oregon volunteers, their stomachs full of fighting, claimed to have killed at least four Modocs. How they had scored their kills while huddled beneath a ledge they did not explain. The regulars offered their own explanation for why the volunteers were leaving: they just wanted "to place the Cascade Mountains between them and the Modocs."

Wheaton decided to move his western forces to Lost River near the Natural Bridge, there to plan a second assault on the stronghold, an assault he would never be permitted to make. He now believed the best way to attack the stronghold was with gunboats across Tule Lake, roughly the same way Captain Jack and his people had arrived after the Battle of Lost River. His officers agreed. Always popular, Wheaton in defeat had risen in their esteem.

Moving the army across Tule Lake would expose the Van Bremer ranch to Modoc raids, a side effect of this military maneuver that pleased almost everyone except the Van Bremers. When they loudly announced that they would have to pull out with the army, no one paid them any attention. They did leave with the first troops, but a few miles along the way their heavily laden wagon became mired. The rest of the troops had one bleak pleasure. They marched past the desperate Van Bremers, making whatever helpful suggestions came to mind, but leaving them quite immovably stuck in the mud.

5

WORD OF THE BATTLE reached Washington, D.C., in late January 1873, when the Electoral College was meeting to confirm formally the election of Ulysses S. Grant to a second term. Among the loyal Republican electors from the state of Oregon was A. B. Meacham.

Meacham went to work immediately. Staying discreetly in the background himself, he arranged for a delegation of Oregonians in Washington to call upon the Secretary of the Interior on Saturday, January 25th. They used the battle to argue that the military approach to the Modoc problem had failed, and that a return to the peace policy was imperative. As one of them put it, "Jawbone is cheaper than ammunition." Secretary Columbus Delano was openly sympathetic. He asked the delegation to put its proposal in writing so that he could present it to the president and his cabinet.

Delano received their letter on Monday, January 27th. The letter proposed a specific means of resolving the escalating conflict: "A peace commissioner should hasten to the scene of trouble as coming from the 'Great Father' of all the people, both whites and Indians, with full authority to hear and adjust all the difficulties." The signers, moreover, happened to know of just the right person for such a commission. "On account of his personal acquaintance with those Indians and their implicit confidence in him, we would respectfully suggest and recommend Hon. A. B. Meacham as a proper man to appoint as a peace commissioner for the adjustment of difficulties with those tribes and the carrying out of the policy herein indicated."

Secretary of the Interior Delano was delighted at this proposal. He had no desire to see a renewed attempt to transfer Indian affairs back to the War Department. He must have expected that Tecumseh Sherman would use the Modoc trouble to make this proposal again. The letter from the Oregon delegation cleverly framed the uprising as a failure of the military; it asserted flatly, "The Indians and military are incompatible." A successful Peace Commission could demonstrate once and for all the superiority of having Interior handle Indian disputes.

The very day after Secretary Delano received the letter he called in Meacham and offered him the commission. After suitable expressions of his own unworthiness and of the difficulties and dangers attending the task, and after Delano had in response expatiated on the importance of the job and the unique qualifications that Meacham possessed, Meacham accepted the appointment. Two other commissioners, in Delano's revision of the Oregonian plan, were appointed in consultation with Meacham.

By January 30th a bitterly resigned Sherman had sent orders to Canby that while the Peace Commission was at work the army was to avoid battle, except in self-defense or to protect settlers.

Canby, for his part, was in no hurry to assault the citadel. One problem was reconnaissance. The Klamath scouts had, everyone agreed, proven worthless in the first fight. Their bravery seemed to lessen the farther they were from their home territory. Canby discharged them as being "insufficient and no longer required."

Canby was sending to Washington for scouts from the Warm Springs Indians who had served the United States military well in earlier campaigns. Better yet, they were feared enemies of the Modocs. Donald McKay would lead them. Canby intended to leak the news that the new scouts and McKay were on their way. He hoped this might induce the Modocs to surrender their stronghold without another fight.

Canby reorganized the command of his forces. He came down from Portland to take direct command. He also decided to replace Wheaton with Colonel Alvan Gillem, who was to arrive from Yreka to relieve Wheaton on February 7th. Wheaton's junior officers were distraught on his behalf; as one put it, "Never since General McClellan had been relieved from the Army of the Potomac did I see such consternation rest on the faces of officers and men."

"Cal" Gillem, as his friends called him, had been a protégé of former President and fellow Tennessean Andrew Johnson. A West Point graduate, he had risen to major general of the Tennessee volunteers during the Civil War, and now he was back to colonel in the regular army. As an officer, Gillem went about his responsibilities with a fussy efficiency that endeared him to his superiors but annoyed those who had to work under him. Gillem's style could at times seem to them like primping arrogance.

Gillem did not help his own standing with his new officers when he mishandled the deeply disappointed Wheaton. He said to him, "Frank, should a fight occur, I will send for you and you can have your half of the chicken pie." Everyone who heard this promise assumed Gillem had no intention of keeping it, and the officers who had fought in the Battle for the Stronghold took Gillem's cavalier treatment of Wheaton as a personal affront to themselves as well. Wheaton himself responded with dignity, "I am much obliged to you for the proposition and will be glad to assist you should a fight occur."

While Gillem was doing his best to offend his officers, the Peace Commission was surviving its own minor crisis. Delano suggested that Odeneal be appointed to it. Delano was a Washington deal maker, always eager to make concessions for the sake of appearances. Appointing Odeneal to the Peace Commission would show, more or less, that the Grant administration did not admit it had made a mistake by replacing Meacham with Odeneal earlier on.

Meacham wanted nothing of this oily Washington reasoning, yet on such matters Delano could be insistent. Odeneal's timidity saved the day. He had no desire to meet with Modocs on the war path. Pleading other business, he suggested the new head of the Klamath reservation, L. S. Dyar, as his replacement.

The announcement of the decision to appoint a Peace Commission was met with considerable bitterness in Linkville. The settlers saw it as the beginning of a sellout. As one Oregonian later put it, "The churches hypnotized the grim soldier in the White House, and the result was the 'Peace Commission.'"

The mood in southern Oregon did not improve when Gillem, discovering that freight cost twice as much to bring down from Oregon as it did up from California, began to get his supplies from Yreka. No profits from the army and a peace probably dictated by Captain Jack and A. B. Meacham! By mid-February when Meacham reached the Fairchild ranch, where General Canby had established his own headquarters, the future looked bleak as a sleet storm.

The Oregonians tried to keep up the pressure by indicting nine

Modocs for murder. Some of those indicted had definitely been with Hooker Jim; others, such as Scarfaced Charley, seem to have been included in the indictment just because their names were known.

In the meantime, John Fairchild and Press Dorris had done what they could to preserve the prospects for peace. They had received a message from Captain Jack through a Modoc woman. He wanted to talk to them in his camp. They armed themselves and followed her and were greeted as friends. Modoc warriors extended their hands to shake.

Fairchild did not offer his in return. "No, you don't, until we understand each other," he said. "We came here because we learned that you wanted to talk peace. We are not afraid to talk or to hear you talk. We were in the battle. We fought you, and we will fight again unless peace is made."

Captain Jack replied quickly that the Modocs knew who was in the battle and who was not. That was not the issue.

"We are glad you come," he said. "We want you to hear our side of the story. We do not want any war. Let us go back to our homes on Lost River. We are willing to pay you for the cattle we have killed. We don't want to fight any more."

This exchange, as reported by Fairchild, seemed to be the best possible news to Meacham when he arrived to take charge of the negotiations. Captain Jack was making his own peace gestures. Meacham sent Fairchild back to explain to the Modoc leader about the Peace Commission, then to ask for an armistice, and to make sure that Captain Jack understood this meant that no acts of war would be permitted by either side while the negotiations for peace were going on. Any such hostile acts, he emphasized, would jeopardize the whole peace process. Fairchild relayed the message, and received from Jack an encouraging response, which he duly reported to Meacham.

According to Fairchild, Captain Jack had said, "I understand you about not fighting, or killing cattle, or stealing horses. Tell your people they need not be afraid to go over the country while we are making peace. My boys will stay in the rocks while it is being settled. We will not fire the first shot. You can go and hunt your cattle. No one will shoot you. We will not begin again first. I am willing to meet the commissioners at the foot of the bluff, but I don't want them to come with soldiers to make peace. The soldiers frighten my boys."

Now began almost daily communication between the two camps. Messages were also sent to Yreka that Steele and Roseborough should come to the army camp to help the negotiations. Meacham needed as many Americans Captain Jack trusted as he could get. In the negotiations Boston Charley and Bogus Charley usually served as messengers for the Modocs, Frank and Tobey Riddle for the Americans. Bogus Charley became a particular favorite of Canby and his staff. They thought his English was better than Tobey's. Boston Charley was a charmer. Only nineteen, scarcely five feet tall and slightly built, it was hard to imagine that this boy was a dangerous warrior. Good humored, obviously quick minded, with an adolescent's impulsive boasting sense of humor, he mixed easily with the Americans.

Canby seemed to be uneasy around the Riddles. He suspected Tobey of betraying the Americans to her people, or at least shading her translations to suit her own purposes. Then there was Frank Riddle, a barely literate squaw man who had named his firstborn after the president of the Confederacy. His mere presence made Canby bristle.

Tension developed quickly between Meacham and Canby over the two pairs of translator-messengers. Meacham completely trusted the Riddles. He trusted the two Charleys not at all, precisely because they were too eager to please. But when he tried to talk to Canby about this, he only succeeded in convincing the general that the head of his Peace Commission, despite his good intentions, was a bad judge of character.

The newspapermen who were starting to collect in camp from around California and Oregon thought Meacham could have taken some charm school lessons from the Charleys. Meacham openly regarded the reporters as nuisances who could do only harm. He did his best to bar them from Commission discussions. For his trouble he found himself cast in their stories as a fat-headed flannel-mouth who liked to hear himself talk but had nothing intelligent to say. One reporter wrote, "Meacham, mullet-headed Meacham sticks to it like a hound dog to a pot of cold mush. So long as the thing pays him Ten Dollars a day, you don't catch him resigning—not much."

A correspondent from the *New York Herald* who had arrived to cover the war quickly concluded that the Peace Commission was "a stupendous humbug" and Meacham a "Macawber politician," writing, "Words fell from his silver tongue like peas rolling off a hot platter."

Such stories only made Meacham more truculent. He was worried by what he called "the terrible storm of opposition to peace in Oregon." He was certain that "an honorable and permanent peace" was possible, but he feared that "a slight blunder would defeat the whole mission."

While the press was casting Meacham as the fool, the California reporters, in particular, had decided that the Applegates, the first family of southern Oregon, were the villains of the Modoc War. The way the settlers had gouged the poor Modocs was the source of all the difficulty, and now one of them, a villainous profiteer, was being named to the Peace Commission. A friend wrote Oliver Applegate, "I see the son of a bitch of a correspondent for the *Chronicle* is still at his abuse." This all proved too much for the Applegates. Oliver resigned from the Commission. The Applegates, their integrity questioned, decided to be spectators as the Modoc War played itself out.

Meacham ignored the slings and arrows from the press and trudged on with the preliminaries for formal negotiations. Through his messengers he informed Captain Jack that the commissioners could not meet with him at the base of the bluff unless they were accompanied by a guard of soldiers. He left unsaid the obvious reason: there was too much chance for ambush. The commissioners, he added, would be happy to meet Captain Jack and his men on open ground, either armed or unarmed. Meacham also informed Captain Jack that he had sent for Steele as well as for Roseborough from Yreka. He had just arranged to have Roseborough appointed to the Peace Commission to replace Applegate.

When the Yrekans arrived, it was decided to use Steele to make an initial offer to the Modocs. He traveled into Captain Jack's camp on February 28, 1873, with Fairchild and the Riddles as well as a newspaper reporter from Sacramento. Steele proposed a concrete deal.

The Modocs could have amnesty, but only if they surrendered as prisoners of war. They would then be taken away—to Angel Island in San Francisco Bay, or to Arizona, or the Indian Territory—there to be clothed and fed at government expense until a new reservation was found for them. They would have the right to approve this new reservation, but it would have to be far from Tule Lake.

Steele was delighted by the reception of his speech. A number of prominent Modocs, including Queen Mary and Hooker Jim, accompanied him on his return to the American camp. In his excitement Steele rode ahead of his party. When within sight of the Fairchild ranch, he raised his hat and shouted, "They accept peace!"

The response among the Americans was immediate jubilation. While Steele was away, Canby had been told by a delegation of Modocs, led by Bogus Charley and Boston Charley, that the Modocs were ready to accept peace on American terms. By the time the whole American party arrived in camp, couriers had been selected to ride to Yreka and elsewhere. The dispatches they were to carry were being written, and a celebration was being prepared. Canby's own message to Sherman was already on its way.

Fairchild put on the damper. "I don't think the Modocs agreed to accept the terms offered. True, they responded to Steele's speech, but not in that way. I tell you they do not understand that they have agreed to surrender yet, on any terms."

An annoyed Steele repeated his assertion.

The newspaperman carefully reviewed the Modoc responses from his notes. They *had* responded to Steele's proposal with enthusiasm— but did enthusiasm mean assent? Queen Mary and the other Modocs in camp were now put on the spot. They became noncommittal. They had come with the Americans to listen, not to talk. This had little effect on the ebullient Steele. He said he would lay all doubts to rest by returning to Captain Jack's camp the very next day to get explicit assurances that no one could doubt.

Fairchild was then asked to accompany him. Fairchild just closed his eyes and slowly shook his head. Of course, Steele assumed that Frank and Tobey Riddle would serve again as his interpreters. Frank said his wife could go—but, no, he himself would not. And for the first time it may have occurred to Steele that he might have been the one who misunderstood.

The newspaperman, for his part, was eager to go back. Another scoop.

The next day it took only a few seconds in Captain Jack's camp for Steele to realize that he was wrong. The greeting he received, he later said, made his "hair stand on end." The Modocs had obviously been mulling over his proposal since yesterday, and they found it more than unacceptable. Captain Jack did shake hands, but only with reluctance. His demeanor was one of deep sadness, almost as if he were in mourning for a friend—who, Steele understood, might in all likelihood be Steele himself.

Captain Jack began their conference by saying that yesterday the Modocs had not yet shown their hearts. His friend Steele had missed some words if he thought they had. Steele quickly asserted that he was their friend and would never knowingly misrepresent them. Schonchin John now erupted. Steele was a traitor who lied about the Modocs, who talked peace but acted with a bad heart.

Steele was no longer thinking about peace, only survival one minute at a time. As for the eager newspaperman, he felt as if he had stopped breathing the moment they entered the camp.

Steele confronted Schonchin, meeting anger with anger: "I do not want to talk to a man when his heart is bad. We will talk again tomorrow."

To his relief the council then broke up. But now he had to make it through the night in Captain Jack's camp. He could see the Modocs standing in small groups, talking quietly to one another. He knew for certain that some if not all were discussing the advisability of his murder.

Captain Jack and Scarfaced Charley then approached Steele and his small party. They firmly informed them that they would be sleeping in Captain Jack's *wikiup* that evening. Steele got no sleep. For form's sake he did close his eyes. Whenever he opened them for a glimpse in the gloom, he could make out the forms of Queen Mary and Scarfaced Charley standing guard.

The next morning the council began again. The general tone was as threatening as before, but Steele had come up with a gambit that he hoped would be attractive even to the most scalp-hungry Modoc warrior. He promised that he would return to Fairchild's ranch and then come back the next day with all the peace commissioners, and all unarmed. The bait was enticing: those who wished to kill him had only to wait a day to kill all the others, too.

After a solemn oath to return, Steele, Tobey, and the newspaperman were permitted to leave. The newspaperman estimated that he didn't start to breathe again until they reached the bluff to the west, about three miles from Captain Jack's camp. He hoped he'd never again have to hold his breath for twenty-four hours.

Steele reached the American camp, explained what had happened, and emphasized that any commissioner who went to Captain Jack's camp would be murdered in short order. Meacham wryly observed, "On his arrival at our camp he looked some older than when he left the morning previous." Steele preferred to age at the normal rate. Soon he was on his way back to Yreka, his scalp more valuable to him than his word.

Oliver Applegate wrote his brother, "Steele barely escaped with his life from the Lava Beds and says when he goes again it will be with a gun."

Probably trying not to think about Sherman's temper, Canby wired his headquarters: "The news from the Modocs this evening indicates a renewal of hostilities, and that they have received an accession of numbers." (Steele reported that he had counted about twenty more warriors with Captain Jack than the Americans had previously estimated.) Meacham telegraphed the discouraging events to the secretary of the interior, and concluded simply: "The mission is a failure." Then he waited for his reply.

On March 5th—it took two or three days to get a response, since the nearest telegraph station was in Yreka sixty miles away—he received the following message from Delano:

> I do not believe the Modocs mean treachery. The mission should not be a failure. Think I understand now their unwillingness to confide in you. Continue negotiations.
> Will consult President and have War Department confer with General Canby tomorrow.

While Delano preferred to pretend the setback had never happened, Sherman was ready to pounce. Apparently without consulting Delano or anyone else, the General of the Army now ordered Canby to take control over the Peace Commission. The time had come for a purely military solution.

The Oregon newspapers had long been of this persuasion. One had urged the Peace Commission to accept any invitation from the Modocs and promised to mourn the commissioners with appropriate solemnity, if losing them would hasten the inevitable: the transfer of the Modocs "to a 'warmer climate'—warmer than Arizona and more suitable to their devilish natures."

While all this was happening, the Modocs were having fun at Canby's expense by breaking their own promises as lightly as Steele had broken his. Queen Mary and Boston Charley were sent by Jack to announce to Canby that the Modocs had decided to accept the terms of surrender. Canby had only to send out empty wagons halfway to the Lava Beds on March 8th; the Modocs would meet them there, to be carried back to the American camp as prisoners. Canby eagerly agreed.

Although Queen Mary did the talking, Boston Charley said to Tobey as he passed her on the way out, "If you ever see me again, I will pay you for the saddle I borrowed." The remark, so typical of Boston Charley, slyly implied she never would see him again. That meant the Modocs would not be coming back in camp. The whole proposal was a ruse. She kept this to herself, however, because she knew Canby did not trust her but favored Boston Charley.

The day before the wagons were to go out, a Modoc messenger arrived to announce a delay of forty-eight hours that would allow the Indians to cremate their dead. Canby agreed.

Tobey Riddle then told Meacham about Boston Charley's crack. Meacham told Canby, who dismissed it: Mrs. Riddle, if not simply so stupid as to be worthless, was either working with the Modocs or with those Americans who expected to profit from the war. The insulting implication was that Frank Riddle was on the side of war because of the income he and his wife were getting as interpreters.

So the wagons rode out, with much preparation underway in the American camp to receive the captives, and with Fairchild once again closing his eyes and shaking his head: "I don't think they will come. They are not going to Angel Island, as prisoners of war, just yet."

In the late afternoon all the field glasses in camp were turned to the trail over which the wagons were expected. Finally, at dusk, the wagons appeared out of the deepening darkness, all empty.

Canby felt he had been trifled with, though he tried to hide his exasperation from his men. But he did confide it to his wife in a letter, writing: "They [the Modocs] are the strangest mixture of insolence and arrogance, ignorance and superstition that I have ever seen among Indians, and from this cause results the great difficulty in dealing with them in any way but force. They have no faith in themselves and no confidence in anyone else. Treacherous themselves, they suspect treachery in everything."

The Riddles believed Canby was the one to suspect treachery where there was none to be found, namely in themselves. They made no effort to hide their sense of justification after what had happened, and that only made Canby look more foolish. Moreover, Meacham openly agreed with the Riddles: "Their warning had been disregarded, their opinions dishonored, their integrity doubted."

Canby started to fray under the pressure. He angrily threatened a messenger, telling him that the Modocs should not trifle with him again if they knew what was good for them. His mood could not have been helped when he received a stinging telegram from Uncle Billy: "I trust you will make use of the Military force that no other Indian tribe will imitate their example and that no other reservation will be necessary except graves among their chosen Lava Beds."

At the same time, the newspapers supported Canby against the Peace Commission. One reported: "The Peace Commission is a failure. Every promise made to the Indians was faithfully kept, every Modoc promise broken. . . . Everything points to war." The view of the *New York Herald* had not changed since it ran a triple headline in mid-February:

The Modoc Murders

Arrival of Peace Commissioners at
the Seat of War

The Modocs Cold-Blooded Murderers

The Peace Commission, not surprisingly, began to fall apart. Roseborough resigned and returned to Yreka. Still, Washington wanted the negotiations to continue. The Commission was reconstituted with

Meacham reconfirmed as its chief, but with a new member: the Reverend Doctor Eleasar Thomas.

The Modoc crisis drew increased pressure on President Grant from humanitarians, the kind of pressure that Grant found hard to neutralize. Delano needed to help him by finding someone whose religious and humanitarian credentials were impeccable. If the Peace Commission failed (as now seemed probable), Delano and Grant could show evidence that his administration had done its best.

A senator of California had obligingly suggested the name of Eleasar Thomas, a Protestant minister from a thriving riverport town just north of San Francisco. Since his arrival in California from the East in 1855, Thomas had made a modest reputation in bringing Methodism to the frontier. The fifty-nine-year-old clergyman was eager to serve.

Delano appointed him without consulting Meacham; he assumed Meacham would not object. Meacham raised no objections since he didn't even know Thomas, except as the publisher of a Methodist weekly, *The California Christian Advocate*.

The Advocate had defended the Quaker policy: "The Indians are by no means void of generous sentiments and . . . a proper fulfillment of pledges, together with kindness of treatment, will invariably secure their confidence and friendship." It had also praised Grant for pursuing it: "President Grant will be remembered in coming years for his 'new departure' in dealing with the wild tribes of the mountains." Nonetheless, *The Advocate* editorially seemed much more interested in advocating temperance and attacking "Romanism." It also fretted about the irreligious nature of places like Yreka; one correspondent wrote, "We cannot say the work in northern California is as promising as it should be; the years of toil bestowed and the little fruit now to be seen is a matter for serious reflection."

Thomas at least looked like a thoughtful man, with his pale eyes deep set and almost lost under bushy brows. He resembled Meacham, dressing in carefully tailored suits, consciously trying to bring dignity to his every act. He was even more bald than Meacham; Meacham still had a small patch of hair on his crown, where Thomas had none at all, giving his head a domelike look that enhanced his permanently earnest expression.

A colleague of Thomas, upon hearing of the appointment, blurted, "Dr. Thomas, you are not going to Modoc country to be killed by the Indians?"

The minister responded simply, "The will of the Lord be done."

On his way north he stopped at Yreka, to preach at both a morning and an evening service, asking for prayers for a peaceful resolution of what he called "the Modoc difficulties."

For the secretary of the interior, the appointment of Thomas was only a smoke screen to cover a retreat. While he showcased the appointment in public, in private he capitulated to Sherman and transferred the future control of the Peace Commission to the military under Canby. Meacham might remain chairman in name, but Canby could dictate its membership, appointing and removing whomever he wished, whenever he wished.

So the Peace Commission, with a clergyman onboard but under Canby's effective control, was going to have another try, in all likelihood its last. While the Americans waited for the new peace commissioner to arrive, Canby tried to increase the pressure on the Modocs.

At one point an American patrol took a herd of about thirty Modoc horses. Canby refused to return them, although Meacham protested that the seizure constituted a clear violation of the armistice. Canby assured Meacham and the Modoc messengers (who also protested) that the ponies were being cared for and would be returned right after the Modocs made peace. Meacham, however, knew that Canby's soldiers were already staking out claims to this or that horse.

Canby also sent out parties to get a better sense of the Lava Beds, obviously preparing for a second assault. He even made a personal reconnaissance. Worse, he used a variety of excuses to move his troops closer. His western force was at the Van Bremer ranch, three and a half miles from Captain Jack; the eastern, even closer, was about two miles away. Both were close enough to each other to communicate through field signals. Moreover, the size of this army was slowly but constantly increasing.

Concerning these changes, Canby wrote to his superiors, "A system of gradual compression with an exhibit of the force that can be used

against them . . . will satisfy them of the hopelessness of any resistance
and give the peace party sufficient strength to control the whole band."

To the Modocs, all this seemed a strange way to make peace.
Meacham agreed, but was powerless. He wrote, "I was instructed to
cooperate with General Canby and in no event interfere with the
movement of the troops. A glance at this single proposition tells the
whole story of the failure."

At about this time Dr. Thomas arrived, eager to be of use. Canby
liked him immediately, particularly his appearance and bearing. Meacham liked him too, but for other reasons.

Meacham had at least one long talk with Thomas before the negotiations resumed. Here was another man of peace. They shared much.
They knew themselves to be representing one of the most powerful
governments on earth in the service of peace and human kindness. Yet
all around them were the preparations for war. Did Canby think that
displaying his cannon and his troops was going to persuade Captain
Jack and his Modocs to acknowledge the authority of the American
government?

Meacham was moved by Thomas's deep compassion for the Modocs,
a people the clergyman did not know at all but whose condition he
thought he understood. They were spiritually helpless, he thought, be-
nighted, and would remain so until instructed through (in Meacham's
paraphrase of Thomas's words) "the great principles of Christian justice and power to recognize and respect the individual rights of others." In Thomas, Meacham could see his own altruism without the tem-
pering it had undergone through hard experience on the frontier.

Soon a new negotiation was arranged. The American party, guided
by Boston Charley, consisted of Meacham, Thomas, Dyar, Canby, Gillem
(Canby's second in command), and the Riddles, now reinstated as interpreters. The Riddles were apprehensive. "Be sure to mix up with the
Modocs," they warned everyone. "Don't let them get you in a bunch."

As the negotiators approached one swell in the Lava Beds, Meacham
saw smoke, apparently coming from the ridge itself. When they
reached the ridge, they looked down into Captain Jack's camp in a low
rocky basin. They saw the Modoc leader, the other leading men, and
about six women all standing around the central fire.

Thomas could barely contain himself. He was the first into the camp. Even Meacham was taken aback by his naiveté. Didn't he realize that this whole place spoke of ambush? Didn't he realize that it had been carefully selected to take the Peace Commission out of sight of field glasses? Did he not notice there were three times the number of men that Boston Charley had promised?

No one else in the Peace Commission shared Thomas's enthusiasm, but everyone knew that to refuse to go through with the council would guarantee an attack. There was nothing to do but trust in Captain Jack's continued good faith and his ability to control his men.

The greetings were cordial enough: a peace pipe was smoked; each of the Americans spoke briefly; Jack then responded in kind. The first hour went well if inconsequentially. But during this colloquy storm clouds were building up, off the lake.

Suddenly Hooker Jim spoke firmly to Frank Riddle in Modoc, "Stand aside! Get out of the way!"

This seemed to be a warning that the rest of the Americans were about to be killed, or so both Captain Jack and Tobey interpreted it. They simultaneously told Hooker Jim to stop it, and Tobey bravely moved into the American group. If they were going to kill them, they would have to kill her too.

Perhaps their resolute actions saved the situation. Then the rain made its own contribution. It burst upon the group.

Canby quickly said, "We can not talk in the rain."

Captain Jack now seized the moment to suggest how little the Modoc thought of this man, this *tyee* who had broken the armistice repeatedly and unrepentantly.

The rain was a small matter to a Modoc, he said. Canby was better clothed than Captain Jack. Yet Modocs did not worry about melting like snow.

Having made Canby look foolish, Captain Jack agreed to his proposal that a council tent be set up on neutral ground for the next meetings. The Peace Commission left with Thomas feeling cheerful if puzzled, and with the others openly relieved.

The council tent was built, as Canby had suggested, about halfway between his camp and Captain Jack's, approximately a mile from each. The site selected was on a level stretch of the Lava Beds, fully visible by field glasses and with no cover for ambush nearby.

While this was being done, the Modocs were permitted to visit Canby's camp frequently. Canby agreed to this to achieve two contrary purposes simultaneously: to convince the Modocs that the intentions of the Americans were friendly and to frighten them with the increasing American military might. For the latter purpose it was thought that displays of mortars and artillery would be most effective. At Canby's signal, death could be rained down upon the Lava Beds.

The Modocs were more impressed by what they took to be further violations of the armistice. By now they had learned that a hundred Warm Springs Indians were joining the army as scouts, led by McKay. They saw the communications flags signaling between the two American camps. Both developments they took to be hostile acts that violated the spirit of the armistice.

One day Bogus Charley abruptly asked, "What for you talk over my home? I no like that. What for the Warm Springs come here?"

He and the others appealed to John Fairchild. Fairchild had no honest answer, except the obvious one that Canby was continuing to prepare for an assault. Since that admission could not help peace, Fairchild chose to remain silent.

On April 5th Boston Charley showed up at Canby's camp. Captain Jack wanted to meet personally with "Old Man Meacham," and Meacham should bring John Fairchild along. Both Canby and Thomas were opposed to this meeting, which pointedly excluded them. They suggested that Captain Jack intended some treachery. Meacham and Fairchild disagreed, appealing to their own experience with the Modocs. If treachery were intended, Captain Jack would have wanted to make sure Canby, the American *tyee*, was there.

When Fairchild and Meacham arrived at the Modoc camp, Captain Jack seemed relieved. To them, he said, he could talk freely. Canby and Thomas both frightened him, Canby because of his military appearance and Thomas because he was an American shaman. With his usual sense of courtesy, Captain Jack did not spell out what he obviously meant—that Canby intended to harm the Modocs physically, Thomas spiritually.

All the trouble, he insisted, had come from Odeneal's original refusal to negotiate with him, holing up in Linkville rather than coming forward. Even so, further trouble could still be avoided.

"Take away the soldiers, and the war will stop. Give me a home on Lost River. I can take care of my people. I do not ask anybody to help me. We can make a living for ourselves. Let us have the same chance that other men have. We do not want to ask an agent where we can go. We are men. We are not women."

Meacham decided he had to be firm. He had to convey a realistic sense of the situation as viewed from the American side.

"Since blood has been spilled on Lost River, you cannot live there in peace. The blood would always come up between you and the white men. The army cannot be withdrawn until all the troubles are settled."

Captain Jack sat quiet for a while. Then:

"I hear your words. I give up my home on Lost River. Give me this Lava Bed for a home. I can live here. Take away your soldiers, and we can settle everything. Nobody will ever want these rocks. Give me a home here."

Here was the breakthrough that Meacham had been hoping for, a substantial concession. He knew Captain Jack and his people could not support themselves on the Lava Beds. But they could work for their friends nearby, like Fairchild. Only one further concession needed to be made.

Meacham said that peace required that the Modocs give up the men responsible for the massacre of settlers along Tule Lake.

Jack was quick to respond: "Who will try them? White men or Indians?"

Meacham had to be honest: "White men, of course." To himself he hoped all the Modoc leader was suggesting was that they be tried by a jury of peers.

But Captain Jack pressed harder: "Then you will give up the men who killed Indian women and children on Lost River, to be tried by the Modocs?"

Meacham saw they were on a new path. It led nowhere. He repeated something he had once heard Captain Jack himself say.

"No, because the Modoc law is dead. The white man's law rules the country now. Only one law lives at a time."

Captain Jack was not done: "Will you try the men who fired on my people, on the east side of Lost River, by your own law?"

Meacham was trapped, and he knew it. Captain Jack had, in effect, conceded that the action on the west side of the river was military, and justified by white man's law. But what of the marauding white group that had fired on a Modoc village without provocation? If the Modocs who retaliated for this attack were to be tried by white man's law, then would the same law try the whites who had provoked it?

Meacham wanted to say yes, perhaps even tried to say yes, but he could not.

He lamely responded with: "The white man's law rules the country. The Indian law is dead."

Even as he said it, he must have realized that Captain Jack understood what the evasion signified. The Modoc leader seemed to expect a flat no. He said:

Oh, yes, I see. The white man's laws are good for the white man, but they are made so as to leave the Indian out. No, my friend, I cannot give up the young men to be hung. I know they did wrong. Their blood was bad when they saw the women and children dead. They did not begin. The white man began first. I know they are bad. I can't help that. I have no strong laws and strong houses. Some of your young men are bad, too. You have strong laws and strong houses. Why don't your men do right? No, I cannot give up my young men. Take away the soldiers, and all the trouble will stop.

Meacham could only say, "The soldiers cannot be taken away while you stay in the Lava Beds." They had reached an impasse, and neither of them could see a way out.

Captain Jack then put his hand on Meacham's arm, a gesture of affection and tenderness and desperation. "Tell me, my friend, what I am to do. I do not want to fight."

Meacham spoke now with the full weariness of futility: "The only way now for peace is to come out of the rocks, and we will hunt up a new home for you. Then all this trouble will cease. No peace can be made while you stay in the Lava Beds. We can find you another place, and the president will give you each a home."

This appeal Captain Jack dismissed, as Meacham knew he would: "I don't know any other country. God gave me this country. He put my people here first. I was born here. My father was born here. I want to live here. I do not want to leave the ground where I was born."

The time for true negotiations had passed. Both realized this. Captain Jack now accused the Americans of bad faith.

"You ask me to come out, and put myself in your power. I cannot do it. I am afraid—no, I am not afraid but my people are. When you were at Fairchild's ranch, you sent me word that no more preparation for war would be made by you, and that I must not go on preparing for war until this thing was settled."

Both Meacham and Fairchild knew what was coming next. Captain Jack was now, of course, going to list the Americans' violations of that truce.

"I have done nothing. I have seen your men passing through the country. I could have killed them. I did not. My men have stayed in the rocks all the time. They have not killed anybody. They have not killed any cattle. I have kept my promise. Have you kept yours? Your soldiers stole my horses. You did not give them up. You say you want peace. Why do you come with so many soldiers to make peace? I see your men coming every day with big guns. Does that look like making peace?"

Now Captain Jack was on his feet, pointing along the lake shore.

"Do you see that dark spot there? Forty-six of my people met Ben Wright there when I was a little boy. He told them he wanted to make peace. It was a rainy day. My people wore moccasins then. Their feet were wet. He smoked the pipe with them. They believed him. They sat down to dry their feet. They unstrung their bows, and laid them by their sides, when suddenly Ben Wright drawing a pistol with each hand began shooting my people. Do you know how many escaped?" Captain Jack was shouting now. "Do you know?"

He waited for an answer. But Meacham had no desire to talk about the Ben Wright massacre. Finally Captain Jack raised his hand and slowly extended his fingers, to show five. Just in case Meacham or Fairchild was inclined to dispute this (which of course they were not), Captain Jack added that one of the five was in his camp right now, an old man.

They were in full debate now, and Meacham knew he had to hold his own. He pointed in the general direction of Bloody Point and asked how many survived the Modoc massacre there. Captain Jack dismissed the analogy.

"Your people and mine were at war then. They were not making peace."

Meacham tried a tactical concession. It *was* wrong for Wright to attack under a flag of truce. But Captain Jack would have none of it.

"You say it is wrong, but your Government did not say it was wrong. It made him a *tyee*. Big Chief made him an Indian agent."

These last few exchanges were utterly pointless, and both knew it. Nothing was served by getting angry over past injustices in which neither had taken part.

Captain Jack now rose to conclude the council.

> I am but one man. I am the voice of my people. Whatever their hearts are, that I talk. I want no more war. I want to be a man. You deny me the right of a white man. My skin is red. My heart is a white man's heart. But I am a Modoc. I am not afraid to die. I will not fall on the rocks. When I die, my enemies will be under me. Your soldier begun on me when I was asleep on Lost River. They drove us to these rocks like a wounded deer. Tell your soldier *tyee* I am over here now. Tell him not to hunt for me on Lost River or Shasta Butte. Tell him I am over here. I want him to take his soldiers away. I do not want to fight. I am a Modoc. I am not afraid to die. I can show him how a Modoc can die.

Meacham could only repeat that his government was strong and would not leave. If Captain Jack did not come out, his people would be destroyed. This, of course, made no impression on the Modoc, who did not even respond. Meacham tried to invite Captain Jack to his camp for dinner. He declined. He was not afraid to go into the American camp, but his people were afraid for him.

As Meacham and Fairchild rode back to the American camp, they knew how wise Captain Jack's people were in forbidding him to go to the American camp. Canby might have found the temptation to seize him irresistible.

Meacham had always placed high hopes on Captain Jack, since their first tense encounter in Captain Jack's *wikiup* on Lost River three years earlier. He had believed in the Modoc's sincere commitment to peace. Now, having spent the better part of a day talking with him, it stunned him to see how much he had changed. The crises of the past two years had matured him as a leader. He had truly become the voice of his people, more than he had been at Lost River or the Klamath reservation.

When Meacham reported, Canby, Thomas, and Dyar were rather heartened by the council. They seized on Captain Jack's concession about Lost River. They speculated that the hotheads responsible for the Tule Lake murders were preventing the Modoc leader from surrendering. They decided to send Tobey Riddle to Captain Jack's camp to privately offer him protection if he led those who wanted peace out of the Lava Beds and into American custody.

As they developed this plan, one can imagine Fairchild sitting in a corner nearby, first incredulous and then just closing his eyes, having decided there was no point in saying anything. The damned fools.

Tobey Riddle went on this mission for which Canby, Thomas, and Dyar had such high hopes, and for which Meacham and Fairchild had none. The commissioners all waited tensely for hours. When she finally returned, they rushed to meet her. At first she would say nothing. She would not even get off her horse. Her eyes were swollen with weeping. Only her husband could coax her in private to tell what had happened.

Upon arrival at Captain Jack's camp, she had asked for a private conference, as she was supposed to. But Captain Jack had firmly refused.

"I want all my people to hear," he said.

So she described to the whole band the offer of American protection for any who wished to accept the surrender terms. The matter was put to a vote. Eleven including Captain Jack voted to accept the terms. The majority voted no and warned that any Modoc who attempted to leave the Lava Beds would be considered a traitor to the people and killed immediately. Captain Jack gave in.

"I am a Modoc, and I cannot, and will not leave my people."

As she was riding out, a man, hidden behind a rock, whispered to her in a voice she thought she recognized, "Tell Old Man Meacham and all the men not to come to the council tent again—they get killed."

Tobey was in despair, and her husband thought she was justified. He informed Meacham, who assembled the Peace Commission to tell them. Canby immediately dismissed, as he usually did, anything from the Riddles. He said the Modocs "might talk such a thing, but they would not attempt it." Doctor Thomas, as always optimistic, argued that at worst Tobey was exaggerating. Dyar and Meacham, in contrast, were more than a little inclined to take her very seriously.

The next day a delegation of Modocs—Bogus Charley, Boston Charley, and Shacknasty Jim—arrived at the American camp to propose a meeting at the council tent. Boston Charley did most of the talking and as usual was articulate and plausible. They were so eager for peace, he explained, that they wanted the talk that very day.

Suspicious, Meacham tried to draw Boston Charley out. While these negotiations were progressing slowly, an orderly entered and handed General Canby a message that had been signaled by flag from the eastern camp. It was a warning.

"Five Indians at the council tent, apparently unarmed, and about twenty others, with rifles, are in the rocks a few rods behind them."

The paper, without any comment from Canby, was then quietly passed to the other peace commissioners. All understood what it meant. Meacham concluded the negotiations by assuring Boston Charley that the Americans could not possibly meet with the Modocs that day. The notice was too short.

The treachery touched Thomas to the quick. He then showed how unsuited he was for the business at hand. He intercepted Bogus Charley on the way out of camp.

In a hurt tone he asked, "What do you want to kill us for? We are your friends."

Suddenly Bogus, who up to that moment had ignored the reverend, was intensely interested: "Who told you that?"

Now the reverend tried to be evasive, but he was no good at it—and, of course, he would never, never lie.

Bogus Charley was persistent and became a bit threatening in his manner.

Thomas then blurted, "Tobey told it."

Bogus Charley now sought out Tobey who admitted nothing. But now both she and her husband felt that, thanks to the good reverend, the Modocs had marked them.

Then, shortly after the Modoc delegation had left, a single Modoc messenger came back. He said it was vital for Tobey Riddle to return to the Modoc camp. Both she and her husband thought she would be in great danger. Meacham himself did not. The Modocs must know, he reasoned, that such an assassination would precipitate a general assault on them. They might be willing to risk such an assault if they could wipe out the whole Peace Commission, along with General Canby. But they would not want to start a general war over a woman, and a Modoc woman at that. Tobey should go to keep communication with the Modocs alive, for what little chance remained of a peaceful settlement depended on that communication.

Canby agreed, adding that at the first sign Tobey was being harmed he would order a general assault on the Modocs. Meacham, as tokens of his confidence, gave her his heavy overcoat to wear, and "Joe Lane," a fine sorrel stallion, on loan from Fairchild, to ride. She finally agreed, but with great reluctance, a reluctance her husband shared.

Their ten-year-old boy, Jeff Davis Riddle, was in camp with them. Saying good-bye to him was almost too much for Tobey. She took the child in her arms, then put him down and started toward the horse— but when she reached it, she hesitated, then turned and rushed back to her son to take him in her arms once again. This she did a number of times before she at last was ready to mount Joe Lane. As she rode out, she bent over to whisper a few words to her husband.

Riddle then stationed himself with field glasses to watch her whole journey. When she disappeared into the camp, Riddle, according to one account, strode over to Doctor Thomas, called him a yellow dog, and told him that if anything happened to Tobey he personally would kill him. No one who knew the excitable Riddle took the threat seriously, but Doctor Thomas did not know him.

On Tobey's arrival the Modocs swarmed around her. They demanded to be told how she knew of their plans for assassination. She first denied having any such intelligence. When they would not accept that, she told them she had dreamed it. Now they began to threaten to kill her if she did not tell the truth.

Her now almost frantic husband could see her pointing back toward the American camp, toward him—and then in the opposite direction— and then striking her breast. He could see she was speaking. He did not know what she was saying, only that she was speaking vehemently.

She was saying, "There are soldiers there. There are soldiers there. You touch me and they will fire on you, and not a Modoc will escape. I am a Modoc woman. All my blood is Modoc. I did not dream it. The spirits did not tell me. One of your men told me. I won't tell you who it was. Shoot me, if you dare."

Captain Jack and Scarfaced Charley now intervened and had her safely escorted out of camp. Reunited with her husband and son, she told the Americans never to go to the peace tent again.

Canby called together his highest ranking officers to discuss the situation, with Meacham listening in as representative of the Peace Commission.

Canby's second in command, Colonel Alvan Gillem, was confident: "Well, General, whenever you are through trying to make peace with those fellows, I think I can take them out of their stronghold with the loss of half a dozen men."

Canby sat poker-faced, worrying an unlit cigar in his mouth. None of the officers who had seen action against the Modocs were inclined to speak. Gillem, who had not, may have realized that he sounded foolish, for he added, "Oh, we may have some casualties in wounded men, of course; but we can take them out whenever you give the order."

Again silence.

Canby looked to Major Mason, the commander of infantry at the eastern camp, who realized that he was being wordlessly ordered to give his assessment. By this time, the bad initial impression Gillem had made on officers like Mason had hardened into contempt. Mason meant to use this occasion, any occasion, to make his superior officer look bad in the eyes of Canby.

"With due deference to the opinion of Colonel Gillem, I think if we take them out with the loss of one-third of the entire command, it is doing as well as I expect."

Now the portly Bernard stood up, walking back and forward, obviously relieved that Mason had spoken up against Gillem. He simply said, "I agree with you, Colonel Mason."

At this point Major John Green entered the tent on some other business and was immediately put on the spot. How many men would it cost to take the stronghold? He was evasive, pessimistic.

"I don't know. Only we got licked on the 17th of January like hell."
Then catching himself, "Beg your pardon, general."

Meacham made his way back to the tent set aside for the peace
commissioners. As he did, he became the object of bitter remarks from
some officers. The commissioners were now regarded as bungling
fools by the professionals. Their dithering was simply postponing the
inevitable.

Back at the tent, Mecham looked at Thomas and Dyar. Thomas
seemed completely composed, as if about to give a majestic sermon—a
man impressively grave, dignified, meditative. Dyar, in contrast, sat
with his elbows on his knees, his faced buried in his hands. Meacham
busied himself with the guttering fire in the stove, adding sagebrush to
take off the chill. Not a word was spoken.

There was a rap on the tent pole at the entrance. Meacham responded, "Come in."

Lieutenant Tom Wright entered. He was one of the golden-haired
boys of the camp. The son of a general, he was on his way to becoming a
general himself at an early age, and knew it. He had a pretty young
wife back East to whom he wrote regularly, keeping her assured he
was all right.

Meacham could see immediately that Wright was angry, with all the
impatience of a young warrior eager for opportunities to prove himself.
After a few pleasantries, Wright announced that he wanted to growl at
someone, and he thought this tent would likely provide him with appropriate victims.

Meacham was half-amused, half-resigned: "All right, lieutenant,
pitch in."

The Reverend Thomas, however, decided that what was about to be
said would be likely to be unfit for his ears. He suddenly remembered
he must talk to Canby. Rising, he left the tent, dignity intact. Wright
now started his growl, which Meacham recorded, expletives deleted.

"Well, why don't you just leave here, and give us a chance at those
Modocs? We don't want to lie here all spring and summer, and not have
a chance at them. Now you know we don't like this delay, and we can't
say a word to General Canby about it. I think you ought to leave, and
let us clean them out."

Meacham recounted the recent conversation in which a loss of one third of the command was estimated as the cost. Wright, however, would have none of it.

"Pshaw! I will bet two thousand dollars that Lieutenant Eagan's company and mine can whip the Modocs in fifteen minutes after we get into position. Yes, I'll put the money up. I mean it."

Now it was Meacham's turn to be dismissive.

"Well, my dear lieutenant, you might just say to General Canby that he can send off the other part of the army, about nine hundred men besides your company and Eagan's. As to our leaving, we have a right to be here, and we are under the control of General Canby. And as to moving on the enemy, General Canby is not ready until the Warm Springs Indians arrive. I am of the opinion that no peace can be made, and that you will have an opportunity to try it on the Modoc chief."

Wright rose and bid Meacham good night. He seemed to Meacham in much better spirits, having gotten his feelings off his chest. A good man, he thought, all in all.

Meacham and Dyar were amused the next morning to find that the army cook assigned to their mess was nowhere to be found, an apparent deserter. Not all the men were as eager to clear out the Modocs as Wright was. Stories of desertions were becoming more common.

Dyar and Meacham set about making breakfast on the campfire. The Reverend Thomas sat nearby, idle. Seeing the two engaged in such a homely activity made them seem more approachable to some enlisted men. A couple of them tried to start up a conversation.

"I say, capt'n, have you give it up tryin' to make peace with them Injuns there?"

"Don't know. Why?"

"Well, 'cause why them boys as has been in there says as how it's nearly lightnin'. Them Modocs don't give a fellow any chance. We don't want any Modoc, we don't."

"Sorry for you boys. We are doing all we can to save you, but pressure is too heavy. Guess you'll have to go in and bring them out."

Both soldiers looked disgruntled at this.

One squatted near Meacham and said quietly to him: "Mr. Commissioner, us boys are all your fre'ns, we are. Wish them fellers that wants them Modocs whipped so bad would come down and do it theirselves, don't you? Have you tried everything you can to make peace?"

Meacham said they had, and no luck. Reverend Thomas then ended the fraternizing by speaking to Meacham as if the soldiers were not present. His tone was one of amused superiority.

"Brother Meacham, where did you learn to make bread? Why, this is splendid. Brother Dyar, did you make this coffee? It's delicious."

A little later Canby stopped by. He had heard about the deserter. "Who is cooking for your mess now?" he asked. Meacham answered, "*Copi nika*." When this simple Modoc phrase did not register with Canby, Meacham translated, "Myself."

Amused, the general asked, "What does Mr. Dyar do?" "He washes the dishes." More amused: "What does the doctor do?" "Why, he asks the blessing." Now laughing heartily, Canby scolded, "Doctor, you must not throw off on Brother Dyar."

All were laughing heartily now. Much more heartily than this small joke deserved, Meacham would think later.

Meacham then made renewed offers to Captain Jack for another peace council. His offers, however, always took into account Tobey Riddle's experience. Let the Modocs bring all their warriors armed to within a hundred yards of the peace tent. An equal number of soldiers would be a hundred yards away on the other side of the peace tent. The peace commissioners and the Modoc leaders could then have a council without either side ambushing the other. Meacham repeatedly made this and similar offers, the Modocs as often turning them down on one pretext or another.

Washington was informed of the stalemate. Orders to disband the Peace Commission and to begin military operations were expected soon. This weighed particularly heavily on Reverend Thomas. Meacham, Canby, and Dyar could all see the inevitable coming. They just hoped against hope. For Thomas it was different. He took their failure personally, as if God were punishing him for a lack of faith. He was absent from the camp for hours at a time, out in the Lava Beds praying. Meacham saw him once and heard him repeating over and over again, "One man with faith is stronger than a hundred with interest only."

On April 10th Meacham had an opportunity to visit the camp on the eastern side of the Modoc stronghold. He would be gone the day.

Largely to cheer up the increasingly gloomy Thomas, he left him offi-
cially in charge of the Peace Commission, not that he expected there to
be any significant business.

While on the other side of the lake, Meacham learned by signal telegraph that a Modoc delegation had arrived at Canby's camp to propose
a new meeting with the Peace Commission. He hurried back, but didn't
arrive until the evening. By then, Thomas had already completed an
agreement committing the commissioners, unarmed, to meet at the
peace tent with five unarmed Modoc leaders.

Meacham was astounded. That was exactly the arrangement he
had repeatedly refused to consider because it was unsafe. Reverend
Thomas, however, brushed aside Meacham's qualms.

"God had done a wonderful work in the Modoc camp."

When Meacham looked puzzled, Thomas explained. He had been out
in the Lava Beds praying by himself, when Boston Charley and Bogus
Charley had appeared, as if messengers in answer to his prayers.

They explained to him that the Modocs "had changed their hearts;
that God had put a new fire in them, and they were ashamed of their
bad hearts. They now wanted to make peace. They were willing to surrender. They only wanted the commission to prove their faith in the
Modocs by coming out to meet them unarmed."

It was not hard for Meacham to guess what had really happened.
The two Modocs had eavesdropped on Thomas. They shrewdly tried to
use religion to get concessions from Thomas—and probably were as
surprised as anyone that they actually got them. But it was no use in
telling Thomas that.

Meacham knew that in Thomas's mind everything boiled down to a
single assertion: "God has answered my prayers." Meacham begged to
differ.

He assured Thomas, "God has not been in the Modoc camp this winter. If we go we will not return alive."

Thomas was sincerely shocked, even a little angered, at Meacham's
lack of faith—but otherwise ignored him. He was so pleased with
Bogus and Boston that he had taken them to the commissary for new
clothes.

Meacham, needless to say, did not sleep well that night. It did not
help that Thomas was sleeping soundly nearby, a peacemaker who fully

expected to inherit the earth and soon. When Meacham arose the next morning, he did not fail to notice that this day—April 11th, 1873—was Good Friday on the Christian calendar.

Meacham and Thomas had a tense breakfast together. Thomas ate quickly, like a man on the verge of the triumph of his life. As he got up to leave, in walked Boston Charley. He had accepted Thomas's invitation to eat at their mess that morning. He used the same plate and cup for his breakfast that Thomas had. Meacham scowled at him, but that did not affect Charley's mood.

Then Meacham began to change out of his new boots to old ones, to spare the good ones damage from the lava.

Charley asked, "What for you take 'em off new boots? Why for you no wear 'em new boots?"

When Meacham said nothing in return, Charley began to examine the new boots more closely, asking their cost. Again he chided, "Meacham, why for you no wear 'em new boots?"

Was this Charley's witty way of telling Meacham that he was not going to be needing those boots much longer?

Meacham learned later that the decision to assassinate the peace commissioners had been reached in the Modoc camp on the night of April 10th, when Bogus Charley had brought back the results of his and Boston Charley's most recent visit to the Americans.

Schonchin John had initiated the debate without Captain Jack present. "I have been trapped and fooled by the white people many times and I do not intend to be fooled again." Everyone should be able to see the true purpose of the Peace Commission, he said. The commissioners were just playing for time. Why? "To get more soldiers here." And then what? "When they think they have enough men here, they will jump us and kill the last soul of us."

Black Jim instantly agreed: "Schonchin, you see things right. I, for one, am going to kill my man before they get me."

A consensus to kill the commissioners had already been reached before Captain Jack appeared. When he did, he opposed it. He tried to explain his strategy in negotiating with the Americans.

"I will hold out for a reservation on Hot Creek or right here in the

Lava Beds as I have been doing. When they see I insist on either one of those places, they will offer Yainax. Then I accept, with the understanding I take all my people, none to be tried for murder."

When few seemed moved by his words, Captain Jack pleaded, "All I have to do is to hold councils and stick to my point. I shall win."

The Modoc hotheads rushed him, put a woman's hat on his head and a shawl around his shoulders. Then they pushed him down onto the rocks and mocked him as "a woman, a white-faced squaw." He was, they said, no longer a true Modoc, the white man had stolen his heart.

Captain Jack quickly threw off the hat and shawl, struggled back onto his feet, and then shouted, "I am a Modoc. I am your chief. It shall be done if it costs every drop of blood in my heart. But hear me, all my people. This day's work will cost the life of every Modoc brave. We will not live to see it ended."

His authority now uneasily re-established at the price of assenting to the assassination, Captain Jack now turned to planning the actual attack. The victims had to be assigned according to rank.

Captain Jack would, of course, kill General Canby; Ellen's Man would assist him. Next in importance was Meacham; Schonchin John and Hooker Jim were to take him. Many were eager to take the shaman, Reverend Thomas; Boston Charley and Bogus Charley, however, insisted that he should be theirs, perhaps as a reward for all their skillful negotiations with the Americans. Shacknasty Jim should get Colonel Gillem, if he came. Black Jim had to settle for Dyar.

What of the Riddles? Here Scarfaced Charley who had been biding his time intervened. He denounced the whole plan as an outrage unworthy of the Modocs. He would be there, but he would take no part, except this—he would protect the Riddles and kill anyone who harmed either of them.

Lesser warriors were put in charge of a plan to lure Colonel Mason from the eastern camp into a similar ambush and kill him.

The Modocs would all carry hidden pistols. But this might not be enough, for the Americans could easily conceal weapons on themselves, as Ben Wright had. It was decided that two Modocs would be sent out with an arsenal of rifles under cover of darkness. They would hide in the lava about a hundred yards away from the council tent. When the attack began, at the signal of Captain Jack's war whoop, they would spring from cover and provide the weapons to the warriors. These two could not be prominent Modocs because they would be missed at the council. Rather, two brave boys were selected, Barncho and Slolux. As a reward, Barncho could help Shacknasty kill Gillem and Slolux could help Black Jim with Dyar.

The planning finished, Captain Jack retired to the company of Queen Mary and Scarfaced Charley. He was distraught.

"It is all over. I feel ashamed of what I am doing. I did not think I would ever agree to do this thing."

The morning of the arranged meeting has come; it is good weather. Clouds are stacked high in shapes that seem to mimic in white the lava beds. There is no sign of fog, no threat of rain. The sun is bright, the air still. Tule Lake is so calm that in places it is hard to tell where the water ends and the sky begins. A perfect spring day. On the edge of the Lava Beds wildflowers are beginning to appear, dabs of blue, orange, and pink.

Bogus Charley (who has returned from the stronghold) and Boston Charley are eager for the commissioners to get started to the peace tent. They insist that Captain Jack and four others are already waiting and are getting impatient. However, Canby and Thomas are consulting in Gillem's tent. This is their council, and somehow Thomas's enthusiasm has affected Canby, though he orders that a careful surveillance through field glasses be kept on the tent.

Frank Riddle seeks out Meacham and pleads with him, "Do not go. I think you all will be killed if you do."

Meacham responds, "Then come to Colonel Gillem's tent and say so there."

Riddle agrees. As he and Meacham approach Gillem's tent, they see Canby outside, apparently conducting routine camp business. He says to them, "Go on, gentlemen, don't wait for me. I will be in presently."

They enter and see Gillem in his bed, quite ill; clearly he is going nowhere today, but he should hear the plans. All the commissioners are there, and Riddle is too agitated to wait for Canby.

"Gentlemen, I have been talking with my wife. She has never told me a lie, or deceived me, and she says if you go today you will be killed. We wash our hands of all blame. If you must go, go well armed!"

Riddle has begun to raise his voice, then catches himself. "I give you my opinion because I do not want to be blamed hereafter."

Now Canby enters the tent, and Riddle repeats his warning under the general's suspicious gaze.

Canby responds matter-of-factly, "I have had a field-glass watching the trail all the morning. There are but four men at the council tent. I have given orders for the signal station to keep a strict watch, and, in the event of an attack, the army will move at once against them."

The pragmatism of Canby now gives way to the piety of Thomas. He launches into a brief sermon about being in the hands of God, and trusting himself to Providence. As for Riddle and his wife, he charitably thinks they are just excited—that is why their opinions are unreliable. Now Meacham takes his turn.

"I differ from you, gentlemen. I think we ought to heed the warning. If we do go, we must go armed. Otherwise, we will be attacked. I am opposed to going in any other way."

Dyar chimes in, "I agree with Mr. Meacham. We ought to go prepared for defense. We ought to heed the warning we have had."

Canby now is getting impatient. These men are ignoring the obvious. "With the precaution we have taken there can be no danger."

If Canby is impatient, Thomas has become emphatically righteous: "The agreement is to go unarmed. We must be faithful on our part to the compact, and leave all in the hands of God."

Canby closes the discussion, "The importance of the object in view justifies our taking some risk."

After the meeting Thomas does a strange thing. He goes to the camp store and pays for some clothes he has bought on credit as gifts for the Modocs. Seeing this, an uneasy thought passes through Meacham's mind. He is settling up accounts because he is not sure he will return.

Meacham needs to settle his own nerves. He focuses his attention on how dignified the reverend looks in his light gray Scotch tweed. He looks over to the general who is splendid in his full-dress uniform.

Canby is once again talking to underlings about things that need to be done during his absence. Suddenly Meacham knows he must talk to John Fairchild.

Finding him, he blurts, "John, what do you think? Is it safe to go?"

Fairchild is eager to be of help: "Wait here a minute, and let me have another talk with Bogus. I think I can tell."

A few minutes later, he returns, whittling a stick. Looking up, he slowly shakes his head.

"I can't make out from Bogus what to think. I don't like the looks of things. Still he talks all right. Maybe it's all on the square."

Fairchild has been no help at all and knows it.

Meacham says, "I must go if the general and reverend do."

Determined now, Fairchild goes back to Bogus, with Meacham watching. Bogus is impatient and cuts Fairchild off. Meacham then sees why. Thomas and Canby are on the edge of camp, ready to start. Meacham hurries back to his tent, finds a pencil and a piece of paper, and quickly scribbles a note.

Lava Beds, April 11th, 1873

My dear Wife:

You may be a widow tonight; you shall not be a coward's wife. I go to save my honor. John A. Fairchild will forward my valise and valuables. The chances are all against us. I have done my best to prevent this meeting. I am in no wise to blame.

Yours to the end,

ALFRED

P.S. I give Fairchild six hundred and fifty dollars, currency for you.

A. B. M.

Rushing back to Fairchild, he handed over the note and valuables.

"Here, John, send these to my wife, Salem, Oregon, if I don't get back."

Fairchild, normally so cool, is not now. Meacham turns to see Dyar approaching. He too has something for Fairchild's keeping.

"Mr. Fairchild, send this parcel to Mrs. Dyar."

Dyar's thoughts are obviously Meacham's, but still Meacham tries to reason with him.

"Mr. Dyar, why do you go feeling as you do? I would not go if I were in your place. I must go since I am chairman of the commission—or be disgraced."

The grim Dyar says only, "If you go, I am going. I will not stay, if all the rest go."

As they turn to catch up with Thomas and Canby, they see another pair who will not stay if all the rest go. The Riddles have decided they will be the interpreters for the Peace Commission. Tobey, unlike her husband, is making no effort at stoicism. She is holding tightly the rope of Meacham's borrowed horse, Joe Lane, as if that could prevent the departure.

Meacham asks, "Tobey, give me my horse. We must go now."

She shrieks, "Meacham, you no go. You get kill. You no get your horse. The Modocs mad now. They kill all you men."

She wraps the rope around her, falls to the ground and between sobs manages to shriek at Meacham once again, "Meacham, you no go! You no go! You get kill! You get kill!"

Meacham feels his own composure starting to leave him. He knows the color is leaving his face, his lips threaten to tremble. Rather than trying to take the horse away from her, he rushes on foot toward the edge of camp, calling ahead to the slowly moving Canby and Thomas to wait. They can see, even from a distance, that the corpulent Meacham is breathing heavily.

He rushes up to them, a bit short of breath but obviously intent on trying one last time to dissuade them. He tries to control himself and puts a hand on a shoulder of each man, an attempt at a friendly gesture that is forced. Then he says, "Gentlemen, my cool deliberate opinion is that, if we go to the council tent today, we will be carried home tonight on the stretchers, all cut to pieces."

Meacham is anything but cool and deliberate when he says this, but at least he is now talking firmly: "I tell you, I dare not ignore Tobey's warning. I believe her, and I am not willing to go."

Canby, with the veteran's disdain of green troops who quake at their first exposure to enemy fire, reassures Meacham as he might a private: "Mr. Meacham, you are unduly cautious. There are but five Indians at the council tent, and they dare not attack us."

Meacham now becomes plaintive: "General, the Modocs dare do anything. I know them better than you do, and I know they are desperate. Braver men and worse men never lived on this continent than we are to meet at that tent yonder."

The general, again soothingly, repeats what he has said this morning, as if Meacham has forgotten: "I have left orders for a watch to be kept, and, if they attack us, the army will move at once against them. We have agreed to meet them, and we must do it."

Thomas acts as the reassuring chaplain: "I have agreed to meet them and I never break my word. I am in the hands of God. If He requires my life, I am ready for the sacrifice."

There it is. Thomas has said what Meacham suspected. He has prayed himself into accepting martyrdom.

Meacham, even more rattled, continues to plead. "If we must go, let us be armed."

Thomas is disdainful: "Brother Meacham, the agreement is to go unarmed, and we must do as we have agreed."

The argument goes on and on, between Meacham and Thomas. Finally Canby tries to end it. "Mr. Meacham, I have had more or less connection with the Indian service for thirty years, and I have never made a promise that could not be carried out. I am not willing now to promise anything that we don't intend to keep."

Thomas agrees, Meacham dissents, and the argument starts again, going round and round the same points.

Finally Canby, losing patience, taunts Meacham: "That squaw has got you scared, Meacham. I don't see why you should be so careful of your scalp. It is not much better than my own."

Meacham dejectedly admits that the squaw has scared him, and taunts back: "But we will see before the sun sets who is the worst scared."

He then returns toward the center of the camp. Gets his horse. Makes Fairchild promise that if he is mutilated he will be buried immediately so that his family will never see the body. Is offered a pistol by Fairchild. Watches as Dyar is slipped a derringer by Oliver Applegate. Accepts a derringer himself from Fairchild who whispers to him, "It's sure fire, it's all right." Ignores a final plea from Tobey.

Then off they all go after Reverend Thomas and General Canby who are about one hundred and fifty yards ahead—Meacham, Dyar, and the Riddles, Frank deciding at the last moment, "I'm a goin' afoot;

I don't want no horse to bother me." As they move out, Jeff Riddle shouts to his parents, "If the Modocs kill you, I will avenge you if it takes a lifetime." This helps no one's mood.

The time is a shade past eleven.

Bogus Charley and Boston Charley have ridden ahead to inform the Modocs that the Americans are approaching. Captain Jack has just expressed his regret at what they are about to do, only to be challenged by Ellen's Man. Retorting, "I do not lack courage, but I do not feel it is right to kill those men." He then says, "If it is the Modoc heart, it shall be done."

Boston Charley himself is starting to feel something like remorse. He confides this to Bogus Charley, who scolds him.

"Kill these men and the war will stop. It will scare all the soldiers away."

It is hard to believe that the clever Boston is convinced by this, but it is too late to change course. The Americans approach. Both these Charleys have the rifles they carried openly from the American camp.

Canby and Thomas arrive first. They are greeted cordially. Canby takes a handful of cigars from his pocket and offers them all around. By the time the rest of the Americans arrive, Canby and the Modocs are all smoking happily. Thomas disdains the vice, so does not participate. Their smoke mingles with the general haze that the sagebrush fire gives the camp. It is almost noon, and the sun glints red through this haze, like a distant, dying ember.

Meacham, Dyar, and Frank Riddle have had their own glum talk as they approached. Riddle believes that if attacked their only hope is to run, which he certainly intends to do. Dyar agrees. Meacham does not. His corpulence makes that impractical. He tells the other men, "If we stand together, we can, with the aid of the derringer, get a revolver for Riddle, and then we can all be armed in quick time." Both Dyar and Riddle are still intent on running. Meacham says dejectedly, "I cannot run; but I will sell my life as dearly as possible."

As Dyar, Meacham, and Tobey ride into the camp with Frank walking alongside them, they all notice that the council fire has been built on the far side of the peace tent, out of sight of the signal station, an ominous sign that neither Canby nor Thomas had noticed. The Modocs now greet the little party with exaggerated cordiality, as if they are imitating the way Americans greet one another. Even before they dismount, Modocs mill around them, wanting to shake their hands, personal greetings that could only be described as jovial.

Whatever doubt Meacham has that an assassination is planned now leaves him. Dyar is quickly down from his horse, looking pale. Tobey, who has been completely quiet for a while, now is off her horse and is tying it to a little outcropping of sagebrush.

For the moment Meacham cannot move. He is, once again, losing his nerve. He thinks of his family whom he may never see again. He thinks of his dead brother's children who are also his responsibility. He cannot make himself dismount, and then he sees both Thomas and Canby looking at him, wondering what is the matter—no, knowing what is the matter, Thomas full of pity for one of little faith, Canby expressionless except perhaps for the slight suggestion of a sneer.

That does it. Meacham dismounts. Although there is still a chill in the air, Meacham takes off his overcoat and secures it to the saddle. He does not tie up his horse, but lets its halter hang free. At the first shot Joe Lane will bolt back to the American camp, or so Meacham hopes. He hopes Fairchild gets back this fine sorrel stallion.

All the Americans have dismounted. A little tactical game is played, although Thomas seems oblivious to it and Canby disdains to notice it. In the forced conviviality, the Modocs keep trying to bunch themselves away from the Americans, while Dyar, Meacham, and Riddle are frequently moving to keep the two groups mixed. All is done with studied inadvertence.

The words from the Modocs are friendly, their manner carefree, but their eyes are intent, alive to everything. Bogus Charley is walking away from camp, rifle in hand. He seems to be looking for sagebrush to feed the fire. This is woman's work: why are there no women here? Some have always been present at past councils. Meacham is certain that Bogus is about to give the signal to attack. But Bogus Charley finds the sagebrush, breaks it off and carries it back to the fire. Can Meacham have so misjudged?

Now Hooker Jim is staring in the direction of the American camp, as if suddenly expecting an attack. All the other Modocs, except Captain

Jack, are soon following Jim's gaze and make no effort to hide their tensions. Are they going to attack? But they seem in a defensive posture.

The Americans are now looking too. Soon in the distance between the rocks they see a head pop up and disappear, a white man's head. Dyar recognizes that it is Mr. Clark. The damned fool is out in the Lava Beds alone, looking for some lost horses.

Boston Charley asks accusingly, "Why for he come here? We no want him."

The Americans do not want him either. Meacham says, "Mr. Dyar, will you go out to Mr. Clark and send him back." Dyar does, and when he gets back, the formal council finally begins, with Frank Riddle translating from Modoc to English and Tobey from English to Modoc.

Meacham begins: "We have come here today to hear what you have to propose. You sent for us, and we are here to conclude terms of peace, as your messengers of yesterday requested."

Jack replies: "We want no more war. We are tired, and our women and children are afraid of soldiers. We want them taken away, and then we can make peace."

Meacham: "General Canby is in charge of the soldiers. He is your friend. He came here because the President sent him to look out for everybody and to see that everything goes on all right."

Jack repeats: "We do not want soldiers here. They make our hearts afraid. Send them away, and we can make everything all right."

Meacham expands: "General Canby has charge of the soldiers. He cannot take them away without a letter from the President. You need not be afraid. We are all your friends. We can find you a better home than this, where you can live in peace. If you will come out of the rocks and go with us, we will leave the women and children in camp over on Cottonwood or Hot Creek, and then we shall need the soldiers to make other folks stay away, while we hunt up a new home for you."

Throughout this almost predictable preliminary exchange Meacham notices how agitated Hooker Jim is. He cannot sit still and moves around distractedly, looking now this way, now that. Then out of the corner of his eye, Meacham sees him with a distracted air lean over and tie Joe Lane's harness to a piece of sagebrush, as if remedying an oversight for a friend.

As the preliminaries are finished, Hooker Jim is patting the horse and speaking soothingly to him, all the while staring at Meacham who returns the stare. This pleases Jim. Jim takes Meacham's overcoat from the saddle—all are watching the two men now—and tries it on and buttons it up.

He says in English, "Me old man Meacham now. Bogus, you think me look like old man Meacham?" Hooker Jim is strutting about, imitating Meacham's waddling walk.

Meacham is eager to defuse the situation and decides the best way is to treat it all as a joke. He takes off his hat and says in the best bantering tone he can manage: "Hooker Jim, you had better take my hat also."

Hooker responds, "No"—and then adds in Modoc, "I will, by-and-by. Don't hurry old man."

Neither Canby nor Thomas appears to register the significance of this exchange, but all the rest do.

Tobey, sitting directly in front of Thomas, stifles a theatrical yawn, and then stretches herself out on the ground, to be out of the way of bullets. Dyar, with a face so rigid it looks like marble, walks slowly toward his horse, and begins fiddling with something wrong with the saddle that he has only just now noticed. Frank Riddle almost simultaneously sees something similarly wrong with the saddle of Tobey's horse; aghast but trying not to look it, he saunters over to take care of it. They have each gotten the body of a horse between them and the Modocs. Meacham now understands that they intend to make a run for it by initially using the horses as cover.

Meacham turns to Canby and invites him to talk. The invitation is emphatic, for Meacham is trying to get Canby to recognize the situation for what it is. For the first time Meacham is certain, by the way Canby looks back at him, that he does fully understand. Now they still have a chance. Canby has to promise without qualification to remove all the troops immediately.

Canby has to lie.

Canby stands up, looking magnificent in his full-dress uniform. His bearing is commanding. His face is stern, as if under great strain. Meacham notices that one of his lips slightly quivers. He speaks.

"Tobey, tell these people that the President of the United States sent the soldiers here to protect them as well as the white men. They are all friends of the Indians. They cannot be taken away without the President's consent."

Canby is rattling on, but Meacham finds it hard to listen. Canby is talking about how in one of his earlier commands other Indians had first distrusted him, but then found him to be their friend. How they had given him an Indian name that meant "the tall man." How he is sure that the Modocs will one day think of him as their friend too. So Canby sits down, having done his duty.

That leaves Meacham and the others in need of a miracle. He calls upon the Reverend Doctor Eleasar Thomas to speak. Thomas, rather than rising from his sitting position, moves forward onto his knees, steadying himself by placing his right hand on Meacham's left shoulder. He begins.

"Tobey, tell these people, for me, that I believe the Great Spirit put it into the heart of the President to send us here to make peace. We are all children of one Father. Our hearts are all open to Him. He sees all we do. He knows all our hearts. We are all their friends. I have known General Canby eight years; I have known Mr. Meacham fourteen years, and I have known Mr. Dyar four years. I know all their hearts are good. They are good men. We do not want any more bloodshed. We want to be friends of yours. God sees all we do. He will hold us all responsible for what we do."

Captain Jack looks completely dejected. Meacham realizes that his men are keeping almost as close a watch on him as they are on the Americans. Meacham thinks they are waiting for the sign to kill, but Captain Jack won't give it. Perhaps, when the attack comes, the Modoc leader will side with the Americans, save them. Captain Jack just sits for a long time, everyone expecting him to speak. Finally it is his turn. He must respond. Instead, he just sits, with hands on his knees, staring at Meacham.

Then everyone starts as Captain Jack suddenly jumps up, turns his back to the Americans and begins to walk away from them. He is trying to end the council. Or is he just going to the bushes to relieve himself? Or is this the sign?

But Captain Jack does not get very far before Schonchin John quickly occupies his seat and demands in threatening tones, "Give us Hot Creek for a home, and take the soldiers away."

At this Captain Jack stops and turns.

Meacham does his best to respond to this barely possible demand, this not completely impossible demand: "Maybe we cannot get Hot Creek for you."

Schonchin: "I have been told we could have Hot Creek."

Meacham: "Did Fairchild or Dorris say you could have it?"

When Schonchin admits no, Meacham tries to reason: "Hot Creek belongs to Fairchild and Dorris. We can see them about it, and if we can get it you may have it."

As this exchange progresses, Captain Jack has moved back toward the fire and is now standing just behind Schonchin who is shouting: "Take away your soldiers and give us Hot Creek, or quit talking. I am tired of talking. I talk no more."

Tobey, who is still stretched close to the ground in front of Reverend Thomas, has not finished translating this before Captain Jack gives a war whoop. Everyone who is not already standing, except Tobey, simultaneously jumps to his feet.

Meacham sees Barncho and Slolux in the distance emerge from their hiding place, carrying down about a dozen rifles. Meacham yells, "Captain Jack, what does that mean?"

Captain Jack ignores him. With his right hand he is pulling out a revolver that has been concealed on the left side of his coat; as he does, he shouts in Modoc, "All ready." Then, cocking the pistol with his right hand and aiming the barrel with his left at Canby's head, he pulls the trigger. The pistol misfires.

Meacham looks at Canby and realizes to his horror that the general has momentarily frozen. Captain Jack calmly revolves the cylinder and points again at Canby, who still just stands there. This time the revolver fully fires, and the bullet hits Canby in the head, just below the left eye—it looks to be a mortal wound. Yet somehow Canby is back on his feet, lunging and stumbling away. Captain Jack and Ellen's Man pursue him. Blinded by blood, Canby trips on the lava, falls hard headfirst, his jaw shattered by the impact. Now his whole face is a bloody mess. Quickly Captain Jack is on top of him, pinning his arms, then plunging a knife into his throat. Canby is still not dead but obviously dying.

Ignoring his death agonies, the two Modocs are stripping him of his fine uniform before it gets too crusted with gore. Barncho now has reached them with the rifles. Ellen's Man grabs one from him and puts a bullet through Canby's brain. Captain Jack and Ellen's Man then turn Canby on his back to get the rest of his uniform off him. Having done so, they start back to the peace tent with Canby's uniform in their arms.

Dyar and Riddle are off and running the moment Captain Jack makes his war whoop. Hooker Jim chases Dyar, firing at him with a rifle. But when Dyar turns and shoots back with his pistol, Jim drops to the ground to take cover—and after that, he largely loses interest in pursuit, although Dyar is obviously taking no chances, scrambling as fast as he can over the lava.

Riddle is pursued by Black Jim. Jim fires his rifle at the fleeing man. He is not trying to hit him, however—only to scare him into surrendering. Jim knows that Scarfaced Charley is likely observing this chase from a clear vantage, and the moment Riddle is hit Jim should expect to be fired on from behind, not a pleasant prospect. Riddle, knowing none of this, just counts himself lucky that Jim is not a better shot.

Reverend Thomas is shot almost immediately after Canby was first wounded. Boston Charley hits him high on his left breast. Thomas drops back down to his knees. With his right hand he clutches his wound; his left he stretches toward his attacker.

He moans, "Don't shoot again, Boston. I shall die anyway."

When they do nothing for a moment, he stumbles to his feet and tries to run off as best he can. But they are only playing with him. They trip him from behind and start to taunt him.

"Why don't you turn the bullets? Your medicine is not strong."

Again Thomas makes it to his feet and tries to run, but now he is able to walk only a few hesitant steps. Once again he is on the ground, this time pushed. He does not try to get up at first, but he pleads with them. They laugh at him.

"God damn ya, maybe so you believe what squaw tell ya, next time."

Hearing this, Thomas makes the effort to get up once again. But again he is sprawled on the ground. By this time Slolux has joined them with the rifles. Slolux puts a muzzle to the prostrate Thomas's head and shoots. As they begin to strip him, they turn him over. Thomas says distinctly, "Come . . . Lord . . ." and is silent.

While this is happening, Meacham pulls his derringer, sticks it against the heart of Schonchin, and pulls the trigger. It does not fire. Quickly he tries again. No luck. He looks down to realize he has only half-cocked the temperamental little weapon. Before he can try again, Schonchin has his own pistol out and is pointing it at Meacham's face. Meacham, just as Schonchin fires, jumps backward into a crouch. The bullet tears through the collar of his coat, then through the vest and shirt near his left shoulder, which is only badly bruised. So close is the pistol that Meacham's beard is singed by the powder blast.

Meacham starts to run backwards, threatening with his derringer, which he has managed fully to cock. He is thinking clearly enough to realize he has only one shot and must not waste it unless he is sure he will hit his pursuer. Schonchin empties his own pistol as he comes; Schonchin, terribly excited, scarcely aims and does not even come close to hitting Meacham. When Schonchin's pistol clicks empty, he throws it down, and Meacham is temporarily heartened, and may even be starting toward Schonchin when the Modoc pulls a second revolver.

Tobey Riddle, as Schonchin walks by her, springs up to struggle with Schonchin, yelling at him not to kill Meacham. Slolux has now left the body of Thomas to help. He hits Tobey across the head with the butt of his rifle, sending her sprawling.

Shacknasty, who has been a spectator until now because Gillem did not come, grabs the rifle from Slolux, calmly says, "I'll fetch him," and sits to take careful aim.

The terrified Meacham tries defiance by pointing to his heart and shouting, "Shoot me there, you cowardly red devil!"

Shacknasty intently lines up the shot. But before he can shoot, the prostrate Tobey rises and hits the barrel away. Meacham thinks this is his chance and tries to leap over a low ridge of lava for cover. As he does, Shacknasty gets off his shot, and seeing Meacham tumble shouts, "I hit him, high up! He is all right!" to warn Schonchin that Meacham is still dangerous.

Meacham decides that if he does not get off his one shot now he never will, and he means to take one Modoc with him. He looks out from behind the rocks, derringer at the ready—and can just make out Schonchin sitting, doing something with his pistol. Suddenly he is blinded by a flash, and feels a sting in his forehead. A bullet from Shacknasty has hit him between the eyes, but at an angle from the right—so that it passes out of his skull over the left eyebrow without hitting the brain: probably a ricochet.

Amazingly, he is still conscious. He can still see out of his right eye through the blood. Meacham fires quickly at Schonchin who jumps up, as if with a huge twitch, and then falls with a thump on the rocks. Schonchin has been hit. But Shacknasty continues to work. A bullet tears through Meacham's right arm, and the empty derringer falls. Another shreds the top of his right ear. Another grazes his right temple. This last completely stuns Meacham. He flops down. Unable to move, he feels his limbs quivering, as if he is in his death throes.

A few moments later Meacham feels himself being stripped. He assumes it is Shacknasty. First his boots are taken, then his pants, then his coat. In trying to get the vest off, Shacknasty rips it, so he tosses it aside. He now is more careful, almost gentle with the shirt, a good one. As he is unbuttoning it, the boy Slolux comes up—and Meacham feels a rifle muzzle pushed against his temple and hears the hammer click. But the muzzle is pushed away roughly, and Shacknasty is saying, "You needn't shoot. He is dead. He won't get up."

Then Meacham hears the voice of Captain Jack in the distance, calling. He cannot make out what he is saying. But Shacknasty and Slolux are quickly up and moving away. One of them speaks, obviously addressing Tobey: "There lies another of your brothers, you white-hearted squaw! Go and take care of him. You are no Modoc."

Captain Jack calls for his warriors to retreat back to the stronghold before soldiers arrive. At the edge of the camp together they look back at the carnage through the gloom. It is early afternoon, but the sky is growing dark with thunder clouds. The naked body of Canby lies stretched out on the rocks, already rigid. Meacham in his red flannel long johns is a few steps away, with Tobey tensely crouching over him. She discovers he is still alive, if barely. About twenty yards away lies the half-stripped body of Thomas, which is convulsing. A tableau from hell.

Looking back at the fruit of his skillful diplomacy, Boston Charley is not quite ready to leave. "I am going to have Old Man Meacham's scalp to put on my shot pouch," he says.

Hooker Jim jokes, "He has no scalp or I would have it myself."

Boston is undeterred at the prospect of a scalp from a half-bald man.

As he approaches the prostrate form of Meacham, Tobey starts to brush away the blood from Meacham's face, as if this care may somehow ward Boston off. Both Meacham's eyes are closed; Boston Charley's left hand is covered with Thomas's blood, the left arm spattered with it almost up to the elbow.

Boston now has a knife out, double-bladed, black-handled—a government-issue knife probably taken off a dead or dying soldier the morning after the First Battle for the Stronghold. Boston pushes Tobey away. She tries to resist, but he threatens her then puts one foot on the side of Meacham's head, and starts cutting where his hair is the longest. For the sake of Hooker Jim, Boston loudly declares that this is the best scalp he has ever seen, so good he thinks he will even take an ear with it.

He gashes down to the skull, making a rough half-circle. He is starting to pull the scalp off when Tobey shouts triumphantly. She is looking in the general direction of the American camp and is shouting, "The soldiers are coming!"

They are not, but her act is convincing. The Modocs start to leave quickly. The slightly wounded Schonchin is being carried off on Meacham's borrowed sorrel. Canby's bloody uniform and the blood-drenched clothes of Thomas and Meacham are tied on Dyar's horse. The frustrated Boston Charley, not wanting to be left behind, rises quickly, without a scalp. He sees Tobey's horse and starts for it. She yells to Captain Jack, who tells him to leave it. With a shrug he agrees. The Modocs disappear quickly within the lava flows.

Tobey is now holding the head of Meacham on her lap, rocking slightly. She is wiping away the blood from his eyes with her skirt, but he cannot see. He can hear her though. She is saying softly again and again, "It stop. It stop."

6

AT ABOUT THE TIME the peace commissioners were approaching the peace council site, a lieutenant was joshing with a private on sentry duty at the eastern camp.

"Well, Hardin, this is the last day of the war, and now we can go home and rest."

Private Hardin liked the young Lieutenant Sherwood and felt at ease disagreeing with him.

"This may be the last day of the war, lieutenant, but I don't believe it. I think we shall have at least one more good battle before the war ends."

Sherwood (laughing): "Nonsense! You must not be such a croaker. We shall have peace today."

Sherwood was walking away, probably still chuckling at the cynicism in one so young (Hardin was eighteen, Sherwood in his early twenties) when the private saw two Modocs emerge from cover under a flag of truce. Hardin called to Sherwood, who returned and saw that the Modocs wanted to parlay.

Sherwood's response was immediate: "I'm going to see what they want."

As was Hardin's: "Don't go, lieutenant, they will surely kill you."

But off Sherwood went, with Hardin covering him from a loophole he had improvised in the rocks.

Hardin watched as Sherwood and the Modocs talked briefly. Then the Modocs disappeared, and Sherwood clambered back, still jaunty.

"These Indians will come again at about twelve o'clock. They wish to talk to the big *tyees*, Major Mason, Colonel Bernard, and Major Jackson."

Then Sherwood, realizing that Hardin was about to go off duty, added that Hardin should instruct his relief to inform Sherwood when the Modocs came back. And not to fire on them.

Hardin was scowling and could not resist saying: "I thought so."

Sherwood (perplexed): "What do you mean?"

Hardin: "I mean they let you go so they could catch bigger game."

Sherwood was once again amused at the teen-aged private.

The bigger game, however, did not appear at one o'clock. When the Modocs returned, there was Sherwood ready to go out again, accompanied by another young officer, W. H. Boyle.

As the two approached the Modocs, they asked Sherwood if Boyle was the big *tyee*. The lieutenant responded, "He will not come." A Modoc suggested they move a little closer.

Sherwood and Boyle parlayed with the Modocs a short time longer, as Boyle later recalled, "to show them they did not fear them." Then they bid good-day and started back for their camp.

Almost immediately the Modocs picked up guns they had hidden in the grass nearby, and started shooting at the two men.

Boyle, the first to realize the deception, yelled, "Run! Run for your life!" And added that they should split up. Boyle cut to the right, Sherwood to the left. Sherwood got about thirty paces before he was hit and down. The Modocs then concentrated their fire on Boyle, continuing long after he was out of range.

By this time a relief party was on its way to Sherwood. Seeing it, the Modocs disappeared. The first to reach the fallen Sherwood was Private Hardin. He asked him if he was hit bad. Sherwood said he was. Hardin could tell from the way he said it that Sherwood knew the wound was mortal.

As Sherwood was being carried back into camp where he would die a few days later, Canby's camp was signaled: "Boyle and Sherwood attacked, under a flag of truce."

The message was transcribed, and brought to the ailing Gillem who without hesitation wrote out a message to be carried to Canby. Before the messenger left the camp, a cry was raised, "Firing on the commissioners!" One soldier looked at his watch. It was 12:11 P.M.

Quickly the companies all fell in. They awaited the order from Gillem to march, but Gillem for the moment seemed bewildered. The officer who raised the original cry from the signal station now was rushing to the center of the camp: "I saw Canby fall."

He stormed into Gillem's tent to find out why the men were not moving. Nobody could hear what was said, but he was soon back to give the order that he said was from Gillem: "March, and deploy from the left in skirmish line." Now the general order was given, "Forward!" It echoed down the line.

As the troops approached the council area, they first met an exhausted Dyar: "They are all killed but me." Then they came upon Frank Riddle: "They are all killed." Finally they saw Tobey: "Canby, Thomas, Meacham, all kill."

She thought Meacham had died, but he had only passed out. When he came to, he realized that he had been left. He could see again, so he tried to struggle up before Boston Charley decided to return to finish the scalping. He was unable to move. He heard a vague sound in the general direction of the American camp, and soon made out faint voices.

"Up on the left! Forward my boys!"

"Steady right. Up. Up on the left, you damned scoundrels."

"Steady right, right. Guide, center."

Meacham now could hear the crunching sound of boots on broken lava.

The skirmish line now marched into camp, up to Meacham, and then right past him and the bodies of Canby and Thomas. The men were staying in formation, fearing an Indian attack.

Now the company doctor was with him, yelling over his shoulder: "Bring a stretcher here. Take Meacham. He's not dead."

Meacham begged to differ: "I am dead. I am dead."

As they lifted him on the stretcher he suddenly felt he was dying from thirst: "Water. Give me water."

The doctor opened a canteen and brought it to Meacham's lips—but Meacham quickly turned away his head. The good doctor had filled his canteen with brandy.

Meacham mumbled an explanation, "I can't drink brandy. I am a temperance man."

The doctor waved him off.

"Stop your nonsense. No time for temperance talk now. Down with it! Down with it!"

Meacham allowed the doctor to pour a good swig of brandy into his mouth, his first drink since he had taken the pledge to please his mother at the age of fifteen. The brandy revived him some.

"Am I mortally wounded?"

"Not unless you are wounded internally."

"I am shot through the left shoulder."

"Now boys, for the hospital! Quick! Lose no time, and we will save him."

"I hit Schonchin in the right side. He fell over just in front of me."

"Never mind Schonchin. We'll look out for him. Here, take some more brandy."

As Meacham drank, the doctor was finished humoring him: "Now, boys, quick! He'll stand until you reach the hospital."

Eight men hustled off with the stretcher, four to carry it, four to relieve them. One of them thought to put his coat over Meacham. As they were leaving the camp, they heard a wail. It was Canby's orderly, who had served him since the beginning of the Civil War. He had found the body. The hysterical orderly was pulled away, and then a coat was put over Canby's nakedness. Then someone decided to take canvas off the council tent to make the winding sheets for Canby and Thomas.

Back at the camp, Meacham drifted in and out of consciousness—out of consciousness when the wounds of his head were being sutured, brought back into it by the probing to trace the path of the bullet through his right forearm. Amazingly, no bone was touched. Then the doctors examined his left hand, which had also been hurt.

One said, "The forefinger must come off."

Meacham was in no mood for an operation. "Make out the line of the cut, doctor."

He did, and it felt to Meacham as if the doctor was going to take off a goodly portion of his whole hand down to the wrist.

"I can't hold still while you do that, without chloroform."

"You have lost too much blood to take chloroform."

"Then let it stay until I am stronger."

The doctor, at once encouraged and amused at Meacham's assertiveness, said to Meacham, "The finger would not disfigure a corpse very much."

The mention of a corpse reminded Meacham of his request to

Fairchild to bury him before his family arrived if his body came back mutilated. Meacham roused himself, "Please ask Colonel Gillem to send to Linkville for my wife's brother, Captain Ferree."

"My dear fellow, the general sent a courier for him hours ago."

Meacham dozed off.

When he came to consciousness again, he made out the voice of Ferree: "He will be blind if he recovers, won't he, doctor?" He heard too the noncommittal answer: "He won't be very handsome, that's a fact."

He dozed off again.

Back at Captain Jack's stronghold there was very little exultation. Hardly any plunder was gained. Captain Jack, however, was given Canby's uniform. Ellen's Man insisted on being given Canby's gold watch for his part in killing the general. The council agreed—a decision Captain Jack resented. It was not a happy council. Hooker Jim was condemned for letting Dyar escape. Those responsible for the eastern ambush were mocked. Everyone was apprehensive.

The Modocs all expected a full American attack the next morning. Curley Headed Doctor led them all that night in a Ghost Dance.

The attack did not come with the light. The Americans did not even seem to be preparing for an attack. Curley Headed Doctor's medicine was working still. The Modocs began congratulating themselves on their brilliant stroke against the peace commissioners. The Americans were now afraid, they would never attack, they would now give the Modocs all they asked. Captain Jack knew better.

"The soldiers will come. Our victory is not complete. We must now fight until all are dead."

By the next night preparations were ready for an assault on the stronghold. The Indian scouts arrived at the eastern camp from Warm Springs. Food for the soldiers was prepared. Guns were cleaned and ready, ammunition distributed.

Meacham was awake now and knew this evening that the men and their officers would celebrate the eve of battle in their own ways. Ferree explained to Meacham that the men had settled on a prank.

The Americans had a Modoc prisoner, who had pretended to defect to them but then had been caught passing information back to his people. His guards were going to fake falling asleep and give him a chance to run. The men were betting on the outcome. Ferree had no doubt. He had already bet fifty dollars that Long Jim would make good his escape.

Meacham had shown his disapproval at such shenanigans—and Ferree explained defensively to his moralistic brother-in-law: "I thought I would just tell you, so you wouldn't be scared to death, thinking the Modocs were attacking the camp."

Still, Ferree thought it was a terrific bet. "Two to one he gets away!"

As Meacham lay awake that night waiting for the alarm that would announce Long Jim's attempted escape, the sounds he heard were those of the officers and their traditional party on the eve of battle. He was bemused that this party did not sound much different from a Modoc war dance. This led Meacham, who was feeling much better, to a little moralizing: the results of these two traditions were the same, although the intents were different.

As he would put it in his memoirs, "In the Modoc camp, the dance and medicine are for the purpose of invoking spiritual aid and stimulating the nerves of the braves to heroic deeds. In the soldier camp the intention is to celebrate the stirring scenes passed, to exchange friendship, to blot out all the personal differences that exist, and pledge fidelity for the future."

He knew what these American parties were like—the telling of tales, the sharing of jokes, the mutual ragging, all the while everyone tossing back whiskey, taken straight. Getting tipsy was enough—no one wanted to fight the Modocs on a hangover.

Meacham understood the tradition, even if he did not approve. He knew the party was breaking up when he heard the men singing the traditional song of adjournment. He could make out the tune, but not the words until they reached the melancholy refrain.

> Then stand by your glasses steady,
> This world's a round of lies—
> Three cheers for the dead already,
> And hurrah for the next who dies.

As the officers dispersed, a few decided to stop at Meacham's tent to assure him that Canby and Thomas would be avenged. Meacham thought about the chasms and caverns of the Lava Beds, and what such a battlefield did to traditional notions of military honor and glory. Meacham wondered too which of the men who stopped by—Wright, Eagan, Cranston—would be the first to die.

Later that night Meacham was awakened by the sound of repeated gunfire, a popping that started out quite loud but gradually grew fainter. Then Ferree stuck his head in the tent, exultant. Long Jim had made his break.

"A madder set of fellows you never saw. I knew they couldn't hit him. I've tried that thing, and it can't be done."

A few hours later, at 4 A.M., the shelling of the Modoc position began. Just before, a kindly veteran roused Meacham and warned him.

"Don't get frightened, and think that the mountain is coming down on you, old man. There goes the signal rocket. Now look out!"

There was no more hesitation about negotiations. Dyar had telegraphed Delano on the assassination of the peace commissioners and concluded, "Peace cannot be made with these men." A few days later Meacham felt strong enough to add his own capitulation: "We believe that complete subjugation by the military is the only method by which to deal with these Indians."

Delano could do nothing but capitulate to Sherman, who was making no secret that the assassinations showed he had been right all along. The East Coast humanitarians Sherman so detested, seeing what was about to happen, began to discuss among themselves how to mobilize on behalf of the Modocs.

Not all on the East Coast, however, were humanitarians. A New Jersey chemist was writing to Delano that the best way to fight against an enemy in trenches was with poison gas.

Gillem's plan for the battle followed Wheaton's with one important improvement. No one expected to storm the stronghold without formidable resistance, so the men were to carry three days' rations. "We advanced," one soldier later wrote, "in single file, each with carbine and sixty rounds of ammunition; in his haversack, each carried fifteen hard-tack and a small piece of bacon." Three days would be plenty of time for a methodical advance with a minimum of casualties.

The forces on the west, under the immediate command of Major Green, and those on the east, under the immediate command of Colonel Mason, were to advance simultaneously. They were then to connect up on the north, between the stronghold and the flow of lava that led to open country.

Gillem ordered Mason to detach his Warm Springs scouts and have them connect with the right wing of Green's force. If the Modocs were flushed in that direction, they would move into an ambush that would drive them back into the arms of the main force.

Portions of the army were advancing into position before the bombardment began at 4 A.M. Those who had been in the First Battle for the Stronghold were struck by the difference in the weather. The morning just before first light was beautiful—clear and balmy, no wind, a moonless sky, a dazzling display of stars.

By these same stars that lit the Americans' way, the Modocs were making their own preparations. Women, children, and the elderly had been hidden in caves—rocks piled up at the entrances to protect against stray bullets or mortar fragments. The men stripped for battle, and then tied rawhide around places on their body that would rub against the lava as they crawled.

The Modocs assumed that the American plan of battle would be similar to that of the first assault. Therefore, they intended to offer stiff resistance to the American advances against their southern flank, to prevent those forces from linking up. Other than that, the Modocs meant to harass the Americans sufficiently to make sure that they would not reach the red circle of Curley Headed Doctor by dusk, assuming that the Americans would then retreat back to the comfort of their camps as they had the last time.

By 10 A.M. the western force passed the area of the peace tent, and still not a shot had been fired. They were little over a mile from the stronghold. The men were increasingly tense, remembering the stories of the last battle and waiting, expecting all hell to break loose at any moment.

A green private stumbled, and his rifle went off. This report was answered by a war whoop from somewhere within the lava. Then the Modocs began sniping, and the American advance stopped.

Captain Jack had sent out a party of eight warriors to try to slow the advance of four hundred men, without sacrificing themselves. Firing and moving, firing and moving, they seemed like many more than eight to the Americans. Only on the right were the Americans exposed; there they took five casualties. Even so, the whole line, not just the right, proceeded with the utmost caution. It took the next six hours to make a half mile. One group of Americans advanced a short way, covered by the fire of another—then the other picked its way up and leapfrogged the first. The Americans meant to take the Lava Beds outcropping by outcropping. The fighting was, as one sergeant put it, "desultory."

The Modocs consistently gave way when pressured. The soldiers became used to this, concluding that if they advanced slowly enough they could do so without risk, or almost without risk. One of the few deaths on the left wing of Green's forces occurred when Private Charles Johnson incautiously looked over a ridge into a defile only to receive a bullet in the brain from the Modoc who was just then vacating it.

Toward the end of the day, Gillem rose from his sickbed to see how the battle had progressed. At one point, he and John Fairchild were standing with a vantage on the whole western side of the battlefield. Gillem was more than a little pleased with himself.

"Mr. Fairchild, this is a splendid day's work. How long did it take General Wheaton to get this far?"

Fairchild paused in reflection, considered the matter, and then slowly said, "General, I do not remember exactly, but as near as I can judge it was about twenty minutes."

Gillem effected an abrupt about-face and marched back to camp. As far as is known, he never spoke another word to Fairchild again.

The only amusement of the first day came from an Irish sutler, Pat McManus, who had decided to take his own close look at the battle. He went to where the sharpest action was, the south flank. Somehow in his enthusiasm he managed to get himself well ahead of the American line. By the time he realized this, Steamboat Frank had realized it too.

Frank treated the cowering McManus to a steady round of rifle fire during the rest of that day. Seeing that McManus had safe cover, no soldier seemed inclined to retrieve him. At nightfall McManus managed to slip away. He was hurrying back to safety while still keeping as much as possible under cover, when suddenly he was fired upon by the sentries.

"Dry up there. It's me! Don't you know a white man on his knees from an Indian on his belly?"

Captain Jack seems to have been shocked when he realized that the Americans were not returning to their camps, but instead were settling down for the night in the Lava Beds. The Modocs would have to defend the stronghold the next day. To make matters worse, the Americans resumed the artillery barrage and continued it the whole night.

During the night the Modocs did their best to unnerve the American troops. They crawled near and began to taunt them. A battle of words erupted in the darkness, the soldiers and Indians calling to each other (as one American put it) "in plain if not classical English, names unfit to print."

The next morning Meacham was startled awake by what seemed to be firing within Gillem's camp. "What's that?" he asked. "Burying the dead," he was told.

Before the second day of fighting, Gillem sent a message to Mason: "We will endeavor to end the Modoc War today. Try and join Col. Green's right. Let us exterminate the tribe. Push when Green attacks."

Mason, however, thought that Modocs were between him and Green's right, and that they had also infiltrated behind his lines. In light of this, he wanted to keep his Warm Springs scouts scattered among his forces. So he failed to execute Gillem's order, explaining that it had been "impossible to effect the junction without weakening the line too much." Closer to the truth was his later explanation, "It was not part of *my plan* to expose *my men* unnecessarily."

Major Green, by his own decisions, showed that he shared Mason's contempt for Gillem's judgment. He and Mason intended to join their troops at the lakefront, cutting the Modocs off from their water supply.

From there they believed they could assault the stronghold with minimum casualties. When Gillem realized what was happening, he explicitly ordered both men not to close on the north, but on the south. Once again, they ignored him.

Both Green and Mason were primarily intent on minimizing American casualties. Their men would advance a short way and then pause to build fortifications from piled lava rock that provided cover for the next advance. By the end of the second day the now-combined forces were within fifty yards of the stronghold. The men then settled in for their second night in the Lava Beds.

Curley Headed Doctor still exhorted the Modocs to rely on the Ghost Dance to protect them. The American troops had passed the red tule rope, however, though Curley Headed Doctor had said this would never happen. Then the American artillery did its work. One cannonball sailed into camp and failed to explode, but when a Modoc warrior attempted to pull out its fuse out with his teeth, he was decapitated. The Americans had not only entered the magic circle; they had blown away Curley Headed Doctor's medicine and killed their first Modoc protected by it.

The Modocs were still trying to understand the significance of this development when a cannonball landed in the central fire. No one was hurt in the subsequent explosion, but the Modocs were so terrified that the Americans in their tiny rock forts could hear screams.

The authority of Curley Headed Doctor was broken. The Ghost Dance no longer protected the Modocs. They could no longer expect the Americans to disappear, nor reinforcements to arrive from their own returned dead. From this moment on, Curley Headed Doctor prudently withdrew to the fringe of the band, little more than a squaw, attracting as little attention to himself as possible.

The failure of Curley Headed Doctor tainted those who had allied themselves with him, especially Schonchin John and Black Jim. They were no longer rivals to be *tyee*. The Modocs now knew they were facing a crisis, and all eyes turned to Captain Jack.

He addressed their situation pragmatically. They were well armed and had sufficient food. They did not have enough water to last through another day of fighting. The ice they had stored in their caves was almost all gone. He organized a group of warriors and told them to slip through the American lines to get water from the lake.

The Americans near the lake were well settled in their six-man lava forts. Three men slept while the other three kept guard. Those standing guard detected the Modocs as they moved toward the lake in the darkness, and fired on them from all sides. The Modocs' only hope to reach the lake had been surprise, and that was now gone.

Captain Jack then convinced his people that their position in the stronghold was no longer tenable. They decided to retreat to the south, along a depression in the flow that took them within a few hundred yards of the American lines. To cover this retreat, a small group of Modoc warriors stayed behind, keeping the Modoc fires lit, shooting regularly into the American position and shouting insults across the darkness—giving the impression that everything was normal within the Modoc camp. This rear guard did such a good job that many among the Americans spent the rest of the night awake, expecting a full-scale Modoc assault.

The Modoc retreat went completely unnoticed except by some Warm Spring scouts. They later said they had heard children crying, but did not think to tell their officers about it. The Modocs, one soldier wrote, "had passed out under the line of troops as ants would pass through a sponge."

Although the Americans did not know it, the Second Battle for the Stronghold was already over. The American casualties were twenty-three—six dead, seventeen wounded. Most of these occurred on the right wing of Green's forces, where the Modocs fought from the ravine in the lava that later provided their route of escape.

A message had already been sent to Yreka: "The Modocs cannot escape. They are in our power. It is only a question of time. We have them 'corralled.'"

The next morning the Americans—still expecting a fight, perhaps hand-to-hand—began their methodical, cautious advance against a stronghold that was now empty. It was almost eleven o'clock before the American forces realized the situation. Gillem then ordered a quick pursuit to the south. As usual, Green and Mason ignored him. Their troops advanced at their usual pace, which was glacial.

They first fortified the stronghold against a possible counterattack.

Then they searched the various caves. They could tell which ones had been occupied from the animal bones that had accumulated on the floor during the siege. The stench was overwhelming. They found two old people who had been left behind as too weak to travel—a wounded old man whom the soldiers shot and scalped, and an old woman who, despite her pleading, was shot by a private at the order of his officer. The officer had asked, "Is there anyone here who will put that old hag out of the way?" and was answered, "I'll fix her, lieutenant."

These two old people and the warrior decapitated by the explosion may have been the only Modoc casualties. One private, displaying what he claimed was the scalp of Scarfaced Charley, was apparently flaunting the old man's hair. The warrior's head, on the other hand, became, according to a sergeant, a source of amusement: "Passing troopers generally saluted it with a vicious kick." A doctor finally saved it, and sent it back to be pickled for the sake of science.

The Americans could now appreciate the stronghold as a defensive position. The cave thought to be Captain Jack's was a kettle-shaped indentation in the lava, fifteen feet across at the top but the size of a large room at the bottom, almost completely invulnerable to artillery and random rifle fire. To the west was a long ridge of rock rent in two along its whole length. The Modocs had maneuvered here under complete cover, while firing from holes that were as good as embrasures. One of the soldiers who had fought in the American forces, when he finally had a chance to look at the stronghold, was amazed at the ways in which the Modocs had exploited it, writing later: "When the natural formation did not meet all the requirements . . . the Indians had constructed artificial barriers of stone about four feet in height as breastworks with loopholes to shoot through."

At the center of the camp stood Curley Headed Doctor's abandoned medicine pole, a four-foot limb of a tree decorated with mink's skin, hawk's feathers, and a medicine bead.

Captain Jack did not expect the Americans to delay so long admiring his stronghold. He worried that a quick thrust to the south might catch the Modocs exposed. So, at the urging of Ellen's Man, he attempted a diversion. He sent a party, under Hooker Jim, on a raid against Gillem's camp. The quartermaster in charge of the camp, however, had posted a guard and armed the civilians in camp. And Green refused a panicky request for reinforcements. So, even as a diversion, Hooker Jim's foray failed.

On his way back to Captain Jack, however, Hooker Jim and his men did come across two young men heading for the stronghold. Eugene Hovey, a nineteen-year-old from Yreka, was making a little money and having a little adventure by carrying supplies between the main camp and the American lines. He had with him a friend. The friend got away; Hovey did not. The friend, as he scrambled, heard Hovey's screams. When his naked body was found, his head had been so completely crushed between two rocks that it was the width of a man's hand.

During the next few days the Americans had only the vaguest idea where the main Modoc force was. It was not that all the Modocs were trying to hide. Small groups of Modocs were sometimes seen at a distance, out of rifle range. They seemed to be taunting the Americans, as if inviting an attack.

One time Scarfaced Charley and a small group of warriors appeared within sight of Gillem's camp. Charley then ran his men through an obviously well rehearsed mockery of the American artillery drill. On cue the Modocs held their rifles on the ground, pointed up like howitzers; then Charley would yell, "Fire," and off the bullets would go in the general direction of the Americans.

The Americans, however, had no desire to be led into an ambush. They ignored Charley. After a few volleys he and his men disappeared in the distant brush.

Meacham now got a visit from Lieutenant Tom Wright, the one who had growled at him before the ambush. He was not growling now. He admitted to Meacham that the Modocs were "hell." Meacham baited Wright, since that was obviously what the good-natured Wright had come for. He had had his growl at Meacham, and now he meant to let Meacham have his fun too. All Meacham had to do was play straight man.

"Where is your two thousand dollars now? Suppose you and Eagan took them in fifteen minutes, didn't you?"

As Wright well knew, Eagan during the battle had decided to charge a Modoc position, only fifteen minutes later to find himself on his way back to a bed near to Meacham, where he was lying, bandaged up and on the mend.

Wright took the sarcasm in good spirit. "Took 'em, not much. We got the prettiest licken' ever an army got in the world." Wright had a hard time talking in any other language than frontier hyperbole.

"What kind of a place did you find, anyhow lieutenant?" It was a question Wright wanted to be asked.

"It's no use talking. The match to the Modoc stronghold has not been built and never will be. Give me one hundred picked men, and let me station them, and I will hold that place against five thousand men—yes, ten thousand, as long as ammunition and subsistence last. That's about as near as I can describe it. Oh, I tell you it is the most impregnable fortress in the world! Sumter was nowhere when compared with it."

Everyone in the tent was by now having a wonderful time, thanks to Wright—and he was obviously just getting warmed up.

Meacham, dryly: "What kind of fighter is Captain Jack, lieutenant?"

Wright exploded. "Fighter? Why, he's the biggest Ingen on this continent. See what he's done. Licked a thousand men, killed forty or fifty, and has not lost more than three or four himself. We starved him out, we didn't whip him. He'll turn up in a day or two, ready for another fight. I tell you, Jack's a big Ingen."

The men in camp admired the Modocs and used them as the basis of their humor. The same solicitous veteran who warned Meacham about the start of the shelling kept him posted about the various skirmishes with the Modocs.

"You've seen a big dog chase a cayote until the cayote would turn on him, and then the big dog would turn tail and run for home with the cayote after him, haven't you? Well, that's exactly what's going on out here now."

Meacham himself was still in serious condition. He had lost almost fifty pounds. The doctors still estimated his chances of survival at less than even money. But his injuries were still the butt of the joking.

"Two to one the Modocs take the camp. By gorry, old man, don't know what we are going to do to you. You can't run. You can't fight. You are too big for me to carry. Wish I had a spade, I'd bury you now until the fun is all over. But it's too late. Can't help it, old man, you needn't dodge. It won't do any good. Just lay still—and, if they come, play dead on 'em again. You can do that to perfection, and there ain't a darn bit of danger of their trying to get another scalp off of you. Too big a prairie about the timber line for that. Boston was a darn fool to try it before."

After Scarfaced Charley did his fake artillery show, the veteran stopped by again, to warn Meacham that the end was near. "B'gin to look pretty squally, old man." A great frown covered his face. "I don't like to leave you, but I'll have to do it, no other chance. We'll come back and bury what they don't burn up."

Fairchild happened in, and the veteran explained to him the plan to bury Meacham until the fun was over. Fairchild wished he'd thought of that: "Bully! That'll do. Just the thing."

Fairchild had been reading the Oregon newspapers, which were blaming Meacham and him, among others, for the deaths of Canby and Thomas. He tried to make a joke of it, but his anger came through.

"Better send some more volunteers down here to eat up the Modocs like Captain Kelly's company did the day that Shacknasty Jim held a whole company for seven hours in check. Damn 'em. If any of these fighting enemies come down here, we'll set Shacknasty Jim after them and then you'll see them git."

No one, of course, was worried about the Modocs overrunning the camp. But when Meacham was strong enough, it was decided that he should be transported across Tule Lake, away from the front. He was accompanied on the boat by his brother-in-law, Ferree, and Dr. Cabaniss, who had treated Meacham on the killing ground of the peace commission. This meant that Meacham came in for constant ribbing. When Cabaniss told a jocular version of finding Meacham still alive amidst the carnage, Ferree saw an opening:

"Say, Meacham, what will you give me not to tell how much brandy you drank the other day while you was on the stretcher at the council tents? It's all right for you to humbug the Good Templars by saying that you never drink, but you can't pull the wool over my eyes. No man ever drank a canteen full the first drink, as you did that day. It won't do, Meacham."

Even when a storm blew up and the boat was in danger of swamp-ing, the two men kept up their banter: Meacham had better realize that playing dead won't work this time. He'd better pray like old Joe Meek to be a good man if he gets saved one more time. Keep the brandy for when we get in the water.

After a tense time, they made it to shore. Meacham's wife was there waiting for him. Ferree presented him to her.

"Well, Ophra, here's the old man. He is not very pretty, but he's worth a dozen dead Modocs yet."

Once again his companions joshed him about humbugging the temperance people. That night Meacham woke up in his bed in the Linkville hotel, and it took him a while to remember where he was. He had been having bad dreams.

Dyar, now safely back at the Klamath reservation, sent a belated letter of thanks to Oliver Applegate: "I am very much indebted to you for the derringer. It helped to save my life. I guess I'll have to trade for it. Must keep it to look at and tell my grandchildren about. I hope never to get into such a tight place again. One thing is certain, I'll not yield my own judgment to that of another man when I think there is such danger."

By this time Gillem was trying to determine where Captain Jack and his people had fled. He had written his superiors, "I have dislodged the Modocs from the Stronghold in the Lava Beds. They are moving southward. No effort will be spared to exterminate them."

Gillem hoped to find them on more vulnerable ground somewhere in the southern reaches of the lava flow. He feared, however, that the Modocs would circle around to make their way back to Tule Lake and threaten the remaining settlers. Finally, on April 20th, the Warm Springs scouts thought they had found them in the southern flow about five miles south of Gillem's camp. In an apologetic letter Gillem reported the discovery on April 21st, 1872, to his superiors: "It may seem incredible that they would have remained so near us three days, undiscovered, but an examination of the field, with the innumerable caves, crevices, and chasms, would explain how difficult it is to find a man who is endeavoring to conceal himself."

Colonel Gillem was having to make too many apologies for himself and his men.

He decided that, before moving against the Modocs with full force, he would send out a regular army patrol to confirm the sighting and to determine whether artillery could be brought up against this new camp. There was a sandy butte a little ways off that might be suitable for howitzers. Gillem chose Captain Evan Thomas to lead this patrol. The captain had seen almost no action up to now. It would be good experience for him. Among the other officers was Tom Wright. Altogether, the patrol had sixty-seven men.

As they were starting to march out, Pat McManus, who had obviously not yet learned his lesson, decided to tag along, not because he expected a fight but just to take in the scenery. He went into his tent to pick up a few last-minute items. When he came out, his horse had been unbridled and shooed away. Tobey Riddle admitted to the outraged McManus that she had done it "for the sake of your wife."

From the eastern camp Boutelle noticed the patrol and asked Mason what was happening. They could both see clearly a force of about sixty men advancing in a T-shape formation—a skirmish line leading, then the long column of men, finally an artillery battery at the base.

Mason explained that Captain Thomas's orders were to determine whether howitzers could be placed on the butte for the purpose of shelling Captain Jack's camp. Boutelle, never one to hold his tongue, blurted out his disapproval.

Did Gillem seriously think Captain Jack would let the patrol get that close without a fight? Did he really think that an inexperienced officer like Thomas with his green men could successfully work against Modocs who had successfully held off the whole army?

Mason did not answer. He just shook his head and said, "Too bad."

So the eastern camp watched the patrol grow smaller in the distance. Then they saw the puffs of smoke and heard the faint crackles that signaled a fight. At two in the afternoon the western camp flashed word—a disaster had occurred. They were to send out a relief party that would meet up with another from the western camp. Mason quickly selected Boutelle to lead it.

Boutelle and his party hurried to the place where the Thomas patrol had last been seen. It had been several hours now since any firing had been heard. The patrol was not there, and darkness was coming on.

Boutelle judged that it would be "suicidal to have gone blundering aimlessly through the lava beds at night."

He ordered his men to make camp and set a strong guard. The rest of the men were to pile rocks, to make a defensive position in the event of a night attack—and then settle down to rest. A little before midnight the sentries intercepted eight men from Thomas's patrol, six of them wounded, as they stumbled into the camp. They had appalling news.

The Thomas patrol had been massacred. All the officers were dead, nearly all the enlisted men dead or seriously wounded.

The two unhurt survivors thought they could guide Boutelle and his men back to the remains of the patrol. Boutelle at once called his men to arms—and, after sending the wounded back to Mason, marched off to find what was left. They searched through most of the night and found nothing. Finally, as the eastern sky started to streak gray indicating daybreak, the survivors admitted that they were hopelessly lost.

Boutelle decided that he could do better by himself. He moved forward alone, scouting the land ahead. As he was doing so, he came across a sergeant from the relief party sent from Gillem's camp. Together, they moved forward carefully. He later wrote:

"The terrain was of irregular lava-rock ridges between which the decomposed rock had formed fertile soil, overgrown by very large sagebrush. In the bottom of one of these little depressions under the sagebrush, some little distance from our second halting place, were Major Thomas, dead, Lieutenant Howe, dead, Lieutenant Harris, mortally wounded, and Acting Assistant Surgeon Semig dangerously wounded, together with a number of enlisted men, all dead or wounded."

Boutelle's thought was of the "fearful ordeal through which these poor fellows had passed—shot down in the morning, lying all day without food, water, attention, or protection from the cold, with the horrible fear of impending death at the hands of the Indians."

Boutelle's camp was only one hundred yards away. All through the night, the survivors had undoubtedly heard his men, piling rocks, shouting orders. Yet no one had called out because they assumed the noise came from Modocs waiting calmly until morning to finish them off. Boutelle remembered, "Their relief when the survivors recognized us can scarcely be imagined."

Boutelle tried to banter with the wounded surgeon.

"Hello, Doctor, how are you?"

"Oh, I am all right, Captain, but I am so damned dirty."

Boutelle asked him if he had been hit bad. It was obvious from the caked blood he had. It was also obvious from his demeanor that he thought he was done for.

"My shoulder here is busted, and my heel down there is all shot to hell."

Boutelle thought the man still had a chance if the bullet had not penetrated the chest cavity. He opened his shirt, and traced the path of the bullet. Jokingly, he told him that he would be three quarters of a man, anyway. Or a little less, for he was going to lose a few inches of heel. The wounds were serious, but they did not look dangerous to the experienced Boutelle.

He told the doctor, who grinned: "Boutelle, do you think I'm a damned fool? I'm a doctor, you know."

But it was Boutelle's prognosis that proved correct. That was not much comfort, though. Years later Boutelle, battle-hardened as he was, could not shake what he had stumbled on that morning.

"The sight of dead men was not new to me. In my service during the Civil War I had seen them by the acre, but the sight of poor fellows lying under the sage-brush dead or dying and known to have been uselessly slaughtered was simply revolting."

Thomas, it was learned, had stopped for lunch without putting out sufficient guards on high ground. Some men had even taken off their boots. Then the patrol found itself under a deadly cross fire from the ridges. Pinned down, the situation hopeless, Thomas had buried his gold watch and announced, "I will not retreat a step further. This is as good a place to die as any."

A number of men, including Tom Wright, were still unaccounted for. Boutelle spent much of the rest of the day searching for them.

As Thomas was marching his men into the ambush, he had complained about not seeing any Indians. "That's when I most worry about Indians, when I don't see them," Wright had warned him.

When they came under fire, Wright led a small group of men to storm the ridge. His body along with those of his men were eventually found not too far from Thomas. It had been hard to spot them in the dense sagebrush.

The ambush was led by Scarfaced Charley. Even he seems to have become appalled at the carnage. Long before dusk, Charley had yelled down to the helpless patrol, "All you fellows that ain't dead had better go home. We don't want to kill you all in one day." The Modocs then ceased firing and apparently withdrew.

The horror of the trip back to Gillem camp was almost beyond description. A "dreadful reaction" had set in—first among the survivors, then spreading to the other troops. The mental state of the survivors could be measured by what happened to the Warm Springs scouts who had been ordered to join Thomas's patrol. They had left the eastern camp to join up, but had missed their rendezvous, and Thomas had decided to push forward without them—a fatal mistake.

After the worst of the massacre was over, the scouts had tried to advance and relieve what was left of the patrol. The soldiers, however, seeing more Indians, opened fire upon them. The scouts showed their army hats and tried repeatedly to convince the men they were friend not foe, only to be driven off.

Now that same panic was spreading among Boutelle's troops, strengthened by the cries of the wounded. Their silence was sometimes worse. Boutelle wrote, "The pleadings of some suffering from peritonitis, the result of intestinal wounds, were dreadful and continuous. When it ceased we knew what had occurred."

A storm blew up, torrents of rain soon turned to sleet. After a short time beards, hats, overcoats, and pants were frozen solid. The night, Boutelle remembered, "was as black as a wolf's mouth."

Back at camp, one officer keeping watch for Boutelle's force wrote, "The elements at that time seemed to be trying to cover this awful scene by one of the most fearful storms I ever beheld."

While Boutelle and his men stumbled forward carrying the stretchers, they could see in the distance the single beacon that had been put on the bluff near Gillem's camp to guide them. After a while, all sense of a hierarchy or command vanished. When a stretcher-bearer became exhausted, whoever happened to be closest at hand had to fall in and take over. That included Boutelle himself.

Boutelle estimated that they had begun to carry the wounded out at seven in the evening. They arrived at the camp at dawn the next morning, about half past six. Almost twelve hours to go five miles.

First light produced its own revelation. As one soldier put it, "What a weird and woebegone sight we presented! The want of proper water for the past thirty-six hours, the scant food and scantier clothing, and the chilling storm had blanched every cheek."

Boutelle remembered, in particular, the eyes of his men, how sunken they were, how aged. He remembered too his men asking each other the same astonished question, in a dozen different ways: "Do I look as you do?"

In later years Boutelle tempered his criticism of Gillem. "It is true that Thomas, a distinguished veteran of the war, had never seen any Indian service and lacked that kind of experience, but experience in hell, even with the fire out, is rare."

Yet the cost of this particular experience in hell with the fire out was stark. Of the sixty-six soldiers on that patrol, twenty-seven were killed and seventeen wounded. The only Modoc casualty was a young warrior shot to death while plundering the not quite dead.

The Americans had a new name for their camp. They called it Gillem's Graveyard.

7

THE SHOCK with which newspapers reported the fate of the Thomas patrol rippled through the headlines appearing in the *San Francisco Evening Bulletin*:

THE MODOC WAR
Another Slaughter
THE SAVAGES IN
AMBUSH
Two Officers Missing
Our Troops Completely
Surprised
Twenty-two of Our Brave Fellows
Killed and Nineteen Wounded
Heroism of Our Gal-
lant Boys
Captain Thomas and Lieutenants
Wright and Howe among
the Victims
THE LAST MOMENTS OF CAP-
TAIN THOMAS
List of Killed and Wounded

Among the headlines in the *New York Herald* were

Soldiers Shot Down like Deer
An Invisible Foe
The Knife in the Dark

The reason for the shock was embarrassment. The newspapermen had been reporting that the war was coming to a conclusion. The assassination of Canby and Thomas meant the end of peace talks and the transformation of Modoc troubles into a purely military problem. The army, having been given a free hand, then took the stronghold. For a moment it looked as if the Modocs, flushed from their cover, were doomed before the superior American forces. It all seemed so clear, but then the loss of the Thomas patrol had shown how determined and formidable the Modocs remained.

When would this ever end?

Tecumseh Sherman did not know when the Modoc War was going to end, but he did know who was going to end it. Sherman selected the successor to Canby before news of the massacre had reached Washington. The new commander was a man after Sherman's own heart, whose army career Sherman had been seeking an occasion to revive.

Jefferson C. Davis was a Tennessean of vehement loyalty to the Union who had never forgiven the Confederacy for having chosen a president with his name. A West Point graduate with a distinguished record, he was also an unforgiving man. Once during the war Davis had a personal disagreement at a hotel with his commanding officer. They seem to have been playing cards at the time, and Brigadier General Davis flicked a card into Major General Morton's face. Morton slapped him. Davis stormed off in a fury, returned with a pistol, and killed Morton on the spot—not the way to recommend yourself for promotion.

Davis had served with Union forces at Fort Sumter. Toward the end of the war, he was a major general helping Sherman destroy and otherwise demoralize Georgia. It frustrated Davis that large numbers of emancipated slaves had attached themselves to his army, thereby undermining its offensive capacity. He marched his army across a bridge, then destroyed the bridge, thereby isolating the emancipated slaves on the other side. When many of them were cut down by Confederate cavalry, Davis had to be removed from command to appease the humanitarian outcry.

From Sherman's point of view, this was a man who knew war and thought clearly about it. Sherman may have had a hand in allowing Davis to stay in the regular army after the war. Davis *was* reduced to colonel. He was also assigned to Alaska, recently purchased from Russia and now a convenient Siberia for the American army.

Now Sherman was recalling Davis, giving him command of an Indian war, and telling him to fight it as he saw fit. This was made plain to

Davis in the orders he received by telegraph from the commander of all the Pacific forces, General Schofield:

> I wish you to study the situation carefully and let me know if possible what is necessary to be done. Let there be no more fruitless sacrifices of our troops. There can be no necessity for exposing detachments to such slaughter as occurred on twenty-sixth. Ascertain who is responsible for that affair. If the troops or the number of white or Indian scouts & guides at the Lava Beds are not sufficient, try to inform me how many more are needed. We seem to be acting somewhat in the dark.

Davis knew before he arrived who was responsible for the slaughter of the Thomas patrol. Thomas had made mistakes, but Gillem bore responsibility. Davis may have heard how Gillem had hesitated before sending out men after the peace commissioners—an inexcusable failure of nerve. By the time Davis reached Yreka he had undoubtedly heard the rumors that Gillem had hesitated again before sending out relief to Thomas. Unforgivable.

Still, Davis had decided by the time he reached Gillem's headquarters that he was not going to remove this incompetent just yet. That would be too easy on him. Rather, Davis would let Gillem stay around to suffer the well-earned contempt of his fellow officers. He would also let Gillem retain titular command of the force, while Davis made all the decisions and generally ignored him. Davis was shrewd enough to realize that treating Gillem contemptuously would endear the new commander to his officer corps and convince them that this war finally had a commander.

He also had studied the response of the newspapers to the massacre. It was nothing that surprised him. The press always made it easy for itself, always ready to score cheap points off those who were making the decisions and taking the risks, much as the press had done back in Georgia, almost ruining his career.

Now the newspapers were having a good cry over the mother of a young officer mortally wounded during the Thomas fiasco. Hearing that her son was a casualty, she took a train from Philadelphia, her home, to San Francisco, from there a local train to Redding, from there a stage to Yreka, from there a hired wagon to the top of a bluff near the

Lava Beds, and from there a borrowed mule into Gillem's camp—all to be with her son, who died the next day.

Yet while the newspapers were wringing their hands over this dedicated mother, they were also having a hoot at the expense of the army, making the dead the butt of doggerel:

> I'm Captain Jack of the Lava Beds
> I'm 'cock o' the walk' and chief o' the reds.
> I kin 'lift the ha'r and scalp the heads
> Of the whole United States Army.

When Davis arrived he was appalled at the morale of his forces. Everyone seemed to believe that the Modocs were invincible and that Captain Jack single-handedly *could* scalp the whole army, if he chose. "I found them laboring under great depression of spirits; their cheerless winter camps, heavy losses, and repeated failures, had doubtless diminished their zeal and confidence."

Davis had wanted to make a quick thrust against the Modocs, but he abandoned that plan for the time being. "I deemed it imprudent to order the aggressive movements it was my desire and intention to make at once."

Instead he retrained the army into a fighting force. This at least allowed him to reconnoiter the Lava Beds for himself. He wrote to Schofield on May 5th that he judged them "very strong but not insurmountable." As for his troops, they were "not now in condition to attack but will be soon."

Then another problem came to his attention. How was he to attack the Modocs if they could not be found? He sent out scouts repeatedly, but all they found were six bodies from the Thomas patrol that had been left behind. So Davis sent out another patrol to bring the bodies back for proper military honors.

This second patrol came back, but without the bodies. The men claimed that the corpses were too badly decomposed to be transported, so they had buried them on the spot. Davis must have suspected that the men wanted to get out of ambush country as quickly as possible and did not want to be burdened by bodies. They had simply disobeyed orders out of cowardice. Davis, however, decided not to make an issue of this, although the patrol deserved a whipping.

On May 7th a supply train was attacked at Scorpion's Point. About twenty Americans guarding four wagons were attacked by about twenty Modocs. The Americans ran off after offering only brief resistance. The Modocs gained three horses, eleven mules, and everything from the wagons they could carry. The rest they burned. Davis must have had a difficult time keeping his exasperation under control.

He made a decision about new tactics. It was no longer reasonable to expect a decisive battle between the collected forces of both sides. Davis had to counter Captain Jack's mobility with his own. The chief action, Davis thought, "will devolve upon the mounted troops who will be called on to operate in small detachments moving rapidly, vigorously and frequently independently from each other."

If Davis was getting exasperated, Captain Jack and his people were becoming desperate. They had no source of supplies except what they could take from the Americans. They were starting to run low on ammunition. Their clothes were tattered. Food they could get from hunting and gathering, but water was at a premium. No streams ran in the Lava Beds, and the Modocs were effectively cut off from Tule Lake.

For water the Modocs had to rely on ice caves that dotted the southeastern portion of the Beds. Rainwater and melted snow slowly seeping through the lava would form ice in caves, under the right conditions. But this ice was quickly used up—and it took another year to reform in significant quantities. So Captain Jack and his people moved from cave to cave, slowly drifting east until they were almost directly south of the eastern American camp.

About this time Davis finally received a reliable report from scouts about the general position of the Modocs. Thinking they were trying to escape, Davis ordered a large patrol to travel south from the eastern camp to cut off this route. Significantly, he chose Captain H. C. Hasbrouck, just up from Yreka, to lead this mission. Neither Hasbrouck nor the bulk of his troops had yet seen action against the Modocs. Obviously Davis wanted men in the field who had not already decided the Modocs were invincible. Also among the troops were the undauntable Frazier Boutelle and the always eager Warm Springs scouts.

Hasbrouck and his command worked south for a day and made

camp at a place aptly called Sorass Lake, an undrinkable puddle of al-
kali water surrounded by smelly mud and sorry shrubs. All in all, a
cruel hoax of an oasis.

Hasbrouck had his men dig wells. All he accomplished was to make
them thirstier. He decided reluctantly that he would have to send part
of his forces back to Scorpion Point for a fresh supply of water.

The next day Hasbrouck and the rest of his command settled in
thirstily to await their return. That night a camp dog began to growl
and would not stop. His master, a teamster named Charley Largerel,
tried to warn the soldiers that this meant Modocs were prowling about,
but they laughed at him. He insisted, and would not be quieted any
more than his dog. So Hasbrouck was awakened. Annoyed, he dismissed the warning as just a civilian afraid of the dark.

Largerel was not dissuaded, and he began improvising a breast-
work around his own part of the camp, declaring loudly, "Let the mules
go to hell. We must look out for ourselves."

Then, out of the dark that was just turning gray, all hell broke loose.

Since Hasbrouck's patrol first arrived at Sorass Lake, Captain Jack
and his men had been scouting it undetected. When part of the force
left for water, Captain Jack realized that this was his opportunity to
launch a surprise attack that would trap the Americans between the
Modocs and the muddy shore of Sorass Lake.

In the first moments of the Modoc attack two Americans were
killed, three or four more wounded. As one there remembered, "Men
rolled over behind saddles and bundles of blankets—no covering however small being ignored, fastened on belts and pulling on boots under
a hail of bullets."

The Modocs ran directly at the American camp, firing as they came.
Captain Jack himself could be made out on a nearby ridge, directing
the action, the brass buttons of Canby's dress uniform showing up in
the faint light of dawn.

The American horses stampeded, heading quickly for somewhere,
anywhere, else. The danger was that the Americans would also try to
cut and run. Hasbrouck was cursing loudly, but also giving orders to
officers. He sent the Warm Springs scouts out around a flank and ordered Boutelle to the artillery battery camped nearby, to get their
support. Another officer was sent with his men to catch the horses be-

fore the Modocs got them. Hasbrouck was cursing his men into good order.

All the while the Modocs were advancing rapidly, confident of a massacre. Now they were within a few hundred yards, firing at will into the American camp. Some soldiers panicked, and three more fell. There was nowhere to run. The Americans finally formed a skirmish line and fired at the Modocs, who were still two hundred yards away from the camp. Then the Modocs took cover, intending to pick off one after another of the Americans during the rest of a long day.

Suddenly a sergeant from G Troop jumped up—Thomas Kelley, let his name be recorded—and shouted, "God damn it, let's charge." So the Americans did. The surprised Modocs then began to retreat until the Americans were shooting at them from the cover they had just left.

Hardin, the same teenaged private who had joshed with the doomed Sherwood, was in the middle of this charge. A friend next to him fell. He stooped to help, only to be told, "Go on Charley, I'm done for." He did.

Hardin thought he was finished a few moments later when he was making his way up a ridge only to be confronted by a Modoc just above him with a rifle. Hardin sprawled backward, dropping his rifle and stunned by what he thought was a bullet to his head, then realizing that he had been hit by the muzzle. The Modoc, out of ammunition, was using the rifle as a club. Hardin now grabbed the muzzle and pulled the Modoc down the incline. The Modoc quickly recovered his feet and pulled out a knife, but by then Hardin had his rifle back and shot him dead.

Largerel, who had been watching the charge from cover, now got carried away. He jumped up, waived his hat, and yelled, "Give 'em hell, boys. Don't let them get away this time."

At that moment, as if on cue, the Warm Springs scouts opened up. They had gotten behind the Modocs. Now in danger of being surrounded and massacred, the Modocs retreated through the line the scouts had set up, killing two and wounding one. But as they were retreating Ellen's Man was mortally wounded, the first Modoc leader to die during the war.

Although they suffered no other significant casualties, the Modoc retreat became a rout. The advancing soldiers captured dozens of Modoc horses and pack animals as well as Modoc powder and ammunition. All this was subsequently given to the Warm Springs scouts as a reward for their role. The scouts also took possession of a Modoc corpse, presumably the one for which Hardin was responsible. They amused themselves with it by dragging it behind a horse until it was unidentifiable.

When word got back to Davis of the battle at Sorass Lake, he was delighted. It had been, he thought, "a very square fight, and [we] whipped the Modocs for the first time."

Davis, of course, was wrong by any ordinary measure. The Modocs had suffered only two deaths—and the Americans had suffered ten casualties, five of them dead or dying. The chief Modoc losses were in their supplies. A more judicious assessment of the battle came from Lieutenant Boyle, who considered it a draw.

Nonetheless, Davis was right and Boyle was wrong because a normal assessment of victory and defeat did not apply to this war. The Modocs had, in fact, suffered a decisive defeat at Sorass Lake. They would never recover.

The Modocs could not survive without victories to resupply themselves. At Sorass Lake, instead of securing new supplies, they lost much of their own. This loss was far more important than the casualties they inflicted. In the Modoc camp, it was obvious that they would not be an effective fighting force much longer. The Battle of Sorass Lake achieved what the Battle of Lost River had been intended to achieve. It broke the Modocs.

This was admitted in a bitter debate that now occurred over who was to blame for the death of Ellen's Man. First, however, the fallen warrior had to be given a traditional Modoc cremation. Normally a corpse would be taken to the regular family cremation site, but that was not practical in time of war.

The morning after his death Ellen's Man was laid out, head to the west, in his best clothes. The body was washed, eyes closed, hands unclenched, arms folded on chest. All this was done by a woman not of his family, and for this she was compensated.

They wanted to build up a large pyre, but did not because they were afraid to give away their location. Much of the traditional ritual had to be compromised. But surely the female mourners of his family cut their hair and smeared pitch on their faces. Then the pyre was lit.

Going up in smoke with the body of Ellen's Man went the Modoc will to fight.

The war party of the Modocs now largely turned against Captain Jack: Hooker Jim; Bogus Charley; the Hot Creek Modocs, including Shacknasty Jim and Steamboat Frank; Curley Headed Doctor. Doctor was not apologetic about the failure of his medicine, nor Hooker Jim about his raid on the settlers that made peace negotiations difficult, nor Bogus Charley about his role in the assassination that made them impossible. They came together to blame Captain Jack for everything.

The Modocs—all realized, though none would say it—were now going to lose this war and be at the mercy of the Americans. What they said instead was that the death of Ellen's Man and the defeat at Sorass Lake were all Captain Jack's fault. In his general's coat he had held too aloof from the action, and had not risked himself in his attempt to act like a white general. They would no longer follow his leadership. They would go their own way.

More than a dozen men and their families packed up and rode off. Captain Jack's territory was now to the east of the Lava Beds; they would try to make their way to the west of them, perhaps all the way back to Hot Creek.

By this time Davis had established his own camp at the stronghold in the Lava Beds. This natural defensive position had served the Modocs well; now it would serve him. Patrols could sortie out from the stronghold to seek the Modocs, then retire with little worry about an attack. These patrols were so large that they could overwhelm any Modoc force that stood and fought.

Hooker Jim's band ran into one such patrol, commanded by Hasbrouck who had already distinguished himself at Sorass Lake. This was bad luck, and Hooker Jim knew enough not to fight. As the Americans prepared for battle, Hooker Jim and his band attempted to elude them, fleeing further west. For three days Hasbrouck and his men pursued until the Modoc force was dispersed in all directions.

No real battle had been fought, but five Modocs were killed in what was a running skirmish. Many women, children, and horses were captured. Hasbrouck intended to continue mopping up, but when he reached the Fairchild ranch near Hot Creek on May 20th, Fairchild told him that a Modoc woman had informed him they were ready to surrender. They wanted Fairchild to lead them in.

Davis, informed of this news, now expected the Modoc War to end in victory very soon. Therefore on May 21st he did what he had obviously been planning all along. He relieved the disgraced Gillem of command and sent him back to San Francisco. He also recalled the unfairly treated Frank Wheaton so that he could be in command of the troops when the final capitulation occurred. Davis knew a little bit about unfair treatment of officers from personal experience—and meant to correct it where he could.

The bitter Gillem had hardly ridden out of sight of camp on May 22nd when the shout was raised: "Here they come!" Everyone in camp jumped to his feet and crowded around. It was Fairchild escorting the surrendering Modocs, sixty-three in all, though only twelve of them were warriors.

A hush fell over the camp as they entered it. The soldiers could not quite believe that these were the vaunted Modocs. They looked so weak and disheveled, an appearance reinforced by the pitch with which they had covered their faces in mourning for themselves as a defeated people. Nonetheless, the rags they wore could be recognized as the plunder of victory. Here what was left of an army jacket, there badly faded calico that had once been a Tule Lake settler's favorite dress.

The Modoc procession moved at a snail's pace. The ponies seemed so gaunt and spent they could barely carry the women and children riding on them. Perhaps some soldiers for the first time realized that the Modocs had been fighting with all their families in the field. Now they could see the cost. One observer was mesmerized by what he called the "trailings" of the Modoc procession: "half-naked children, aged squaws who could scarcely hobble, blind, lame, halt, bony."

The procession stopped in the middle of the camp. No one spoke. Then Colonel Davis came out of his tent. He marched the fifty paces that separated them. Davis was introduced to Bogus Charley, who acted as spokesman. Bogus Charley smiled hopefully at Davis, who did not smile back. But when Bogus offered his hand, Davis accepted it.

Then each warrior in succession stepped forward and placed his rifle at Davis's feet.

Davis gave a little speech that was far from welcoming. He warned them that it would go hard on them if they hadn't given up all their weapons. He also threatened them. If they changed their mind and tried to escape, he said, "you will be shot dead." Then he abruptly directed them to a small stand of cottonwoods where they could make camp.

Bogus Charley could not allow the moment to pass without some attempt to ingratiate himself to the American leader. He explained in detail how the group had repudiated Captain Jack and his policies in order to make peace. He also practiced a little deception. He earnestly explained that his friend Boston Charley was not with them because he had been killed in battle, as had Hooker Jim. Curley Headed Doctor, Steamboat Frank, and Shacknasty Jim all confirmed by gestures that Bogus was telling the truth.

Davis brought these leaders back to his tent to interrogate them further. As he was talking with them, he heard a scuffle outside his tent. In burst the recently deceased Hooker Jim who threw himself at Davis's feet. The sight of this prostrate enemy pleased Davis mightily, and he helped him up.

"Here was a man, an outlaw to every human being on earth, throwing down his rifle and saying 'Me, Hooker Jim, me give up.' He stood before me as stolid as bronze. I have seen many grand sights, but taking everything into consideration, that was the grandest sight I ever witnessed."

The Modocs quickly settled in. They seemed docile. The Warm Springs scouts did their best to encourage this transformation by making sure their knives were as sharp as possible—and talking loudly about scalps.

Hooker Jim and Bogus Charley soon made a startling offer to Davis. They, with Steamboat Frank and Shacknasty Jim, would lead the army to Captain Jack. Davis decided they could be trusted, agreed to pay them $100 a month, and sent a message to his commander, General Schofield: "I hope to end the Modoc War soon."

Using horses borrowed from Fairchild, the four "Modoc hounds," as they were being called around camp, led a large army patrol to the east of the Lava Beds where they thought Captain Jack and his few remaining supporters would be hiding. When they reached the general area a couple of days later, Davis had the patrol set up camp and allowed the four Modocs to go off on their own with a few days' rations to find Captain Jack. They were to try to convince him to surrender; if that failed, they were to return to Davis with exact information about his location and strength. No one seemed to have noticed the irony that Hooker Jim and the rest had inherited the job of peace commissioners.

They located Captain Jack without too much trouble. The sentries he had posted intercepted them and led them to within sight of the camp and then left them. They rode in nervously, for all the Modoc warriors in camp, except Captain Jack, had put themselves in a battle line, and looked none too friendly.

When Captain Jack emerged from his *wikiup,* he informed them coldly that they were not going to be treated as friends. They would have to give up their arms if they wished to stay in his camp. Hooker Jim responded by refusing, and the other three made no motion to surrender their weapons; Captain Jack did not insist. He had lost the first battle of wills.

Now he asked why they had come. Before they could answer he recognized their horses as Fairchild's. He knew immediately that they would not steal from Fairchild. Where did they get the horses, he wanted to know. Did the Americans send them to find him?

He was told forthrightly that Hooker Jim's band had surrendered and was advised that now he should surrender too. At this Captain Jack erupted. It was one thing for these men to have left him because they disapproved of his conduct of the war; it was another to use that as a pretext for surrender, especially when they had frustrated his own efforts to negotiate a peace.

Captain Jack said simply he would never surrender; he would die with a gun in his hand like a warrior; he would not die with a rope around his neck. They could become white at heart if they wished; but he, if he ever saw them again, would shoot them. They were no better than dogs.

The Modoc peace commissioners were left speechless. After a tense pause, Bogus Charley meekly asked Captain Jack if he would step away for a few moments so that they could confer with the other Modocs out of his hearing. Again, Captain Jack erupted. No, he would not step away so the traitors could confer. Rather they should leave while they were still alive.

Now Scarfaced Charley stepped in. He wanted to talk with the emissaries, he said. He was tired of fighting, tired of being chased around, tired of living like a dog.

Bogus Charley, encouraged, tried to make the decisive argument. A large body of soldiers, with the Warm Springs scouts, was nearby; they had been ordered to hunt down Captain Jack and his men and they would quickly do so if the Modocs did not surrender now.

Bogus had misjudged. Rather than convincing them, the argument instead turned the mood of the meeting once again to murder. Bogus was immediately challenged. Were he and the rest really there to spy for the soldiers? It took all of Bogus Charley's glibness to dance around this question without answering it.

The emissaries left the camp soon after, with nothing decided. They went quickly back to Davis. They told him where Captain Jack was, and said that he had at most twenty-four warriors still loyal to him.

As Davis and his men approached the canyon in which the Modocs had last seen Captain Jack and his people, Davis divided his forces into three groups, in part because the Modocs had been warning them that Captain Jack's only chance was an ambush. Hooker Jim and one group of troops were to go up the left side of the canyon; Steamboat Frank and the rest of the regular troops were to go up the right; the Warm Spring scouts and Bogus Charley were to go up the center, these last being accompanied by Fairchild who had tagged along because he thought Captain Jack would want to surrender to a white man he trusted. The surgeon, Dr. Cabaniss, also was with this central group.

The Fairchild group had gotten to a few hundred yards from where the Modoc said Captain Jack was camped when they were challenged by three men. They were told to stop and then asked why they had come with so many men. The boyish voice was instantly recognizable; it was Boston Charley back from the dead.

Charley laid down his rifle, as did Fairchild and the Warm Springs scouts. Boston was intent on negotiating a surrender, though of how many Modocs no one was sure. Then a shot rang out, and everyone ducked for cover. Over on the side of the canyon Steamboat Frank had been trying to steady a nervous horse, and the brush had caught in his rifle, causing it to discharge.

The Modocs nearby, whose surrender Bogus Charley had been trying to negotiate, naturally assumed that he had been shot, and did not pause to find out if their assumption was correct. Off they went from their cover in every direction like flushed quail.

Boston Charley promised to try to bring them back and left with Fairchild's blessing. But Charley had not gone far before he ran into the troops on the left, who knew nothing except that a shot had been fired and Charley was a good candidate for the title of Modoc sniper. They seized Charley against his earnest protestations. The Modoc War seemed to be ending in slapstick.

Fairchild waited for more than an hour before sending out a scout to see what was happening. Eventually Charley was freed, and by dark he returned to Fairchild with the fruits of his belated labors. The warriors were all gone, but he did bring in a sizable number of women and children, including Queen Mary.

The next day Fairchild and his men pressed forward, and by the afternoon they found fresh tracks. Then they saw a few Modocs in the distance, who acknowledged their call but then raced away. Later they saw some more Indians, a larger group—but again they ran away. Finally, the Warm Springs scouts located Captain Jack's new hiding place. (He was now down to thirteen men.) As they approached, however, Captain Jack fired warning shots, and the scouts prudently decided to stay at a long distance.

But even at this distance negotiations were possible. Out from cover came Scarfaced Charley. He talked to Dr. Cabaniss; he assured him that the Modocs wanted to surrender. Cabaniss accompanied him back to Captain Jack and his remaining people. He saw firsthand how tired and hungry they were. Captain Jack, in particular, looked spent. As Cabaniss recollected it, the meeting at first was inconsequential.

"I found the chieftain sitting on a rock, a white blanket around him and a carbine by his side. We shook hands, but he was very dignified and had little to say."

After a while Captain Jack began to confide that his people were exhausted and hungry. He asked what would be done to him if he surrendered. Cabaniss did not know, and refused to lie. Not having gotten the assurances he wanted, Captain Jack promised to surrender, but not quite yet. It was already getting late, he said, and the women would rest more comfortably here. He would surrender at first light.

Cabaniss now thought he understood Captain Jack's initial reticence. He knew he had to surrender, but could not bear to do it just yet. He had drawn the discussion out to have one last night of freedom.

As he left, Cabaniss loudly assured Captain Jack, so that all could hear, that there was plenty of food and clothing for them in the American camp, and he would bring some tomorrow morning.

When he came back the next day, he did bring the supplies. He informed the Modocs that the army had pulled back a few miles, as a gesture of good faith. By the time Cabaniss had distributed the goods, it was too late to make for the American camp; so he settled down for the night among the defeated Modocs.

When he awoke from his sound sleep the next morning, the Modocs were still there, except for Captain Jack and a few others. He had told his men he was going out early that morning to look for a better campsite, higher up. Of course, everyone knew they would not need one. Captain Jack simply did not know how to surrender.

On May 29, 1873, Cabaniss led the Modocs back to the American camp, and the eastern Modoc band of warriors repeated the same ceremony of surrender that had been enacted by Hooker Jim's warriors in the west just a week before. The first to place his weapon at the feet of the American commander was Scarfaced Charley, who looked dignified but relieved. Ten or eleven more followed him, including Schonchin John, whose look, one observer thought, combined defiance and despair.

On June 1st Fairchild and an escort began to head back with these prisoners to the main camp of the army under Colonel Davis. That same day a patrol under Major Trimble found Captain Jack's trail; he had eluded them before by doubling back. They quickly set off in pursuit and found that the trail led directly to the camp in which Bogus Charley and the rest had originally found him. The trail was easy to follow. Captain Jack and his few remaining followers were not taking normal precautions.

As the Americans were working themselves along, a Modoc suddenly appeared from cover. It was Humpy Joe, Captain Jack's brother.

Joe demanded to see Fairchild, and Trimble had to say he was not available. Realizing that Captain Jack wanted to surrender to Fairchild and that could mean a delay of days, Trimble issued an ultimatum. Captain Jack should realize that he was surrounded, and that he should surrender before any more lives were lost.

Humpy Joe said, "S'pose let me go. Three day, I get Jack."

One of the men snapped, "Hell, no, we want him now."

Humpy Joe led Trimble by himself back into the brush a short way, then called loudly for Captain Jack. No answer. Then there was the Modoc, standing on a ledge above them, with his rifle. Trimble was at his mercy. Captain Jack also asked for Fairchild, and Trimble repeated that he was not available. Captain Jack climbed down from the ledge, and handed Trimble the rifle. With a somewhat apologetic look, he said his legs had given out.

Trimble led Captain Jack back to the camp. He had never seen him before, so he wasn't sure if this was just another Indian trick to allow the true leader to escape. When Captain Jack's identity was confirmed, Trimble, one of his sergeants later wrote, "threw his hat in the air and cheered like a good fellow. We all followed suit. The cheer was taken up . . . and there was considerable noise."

The sergeant could understand why Trimble at first was skeptical. Captain Jack, he wrote, "looks rather younger than I thought he was, although he is only a passable looking buck and don't at all look the character."

With Captain Jack, Humpy Joe surrendered as well as one or two other men, three women, and a number of small children. This group included Captain Jack's two wives and a young girl who was his daughter.

The Warm Springs scouts led the triumphal procession back to Davis's camp—singing a victory song all the way. If Captain Jack understood what they were singing or even heard it, he gave no acknowledgment. As he rode into camp, the soldiers lined up eagerly along the route to get a look. The Modoc seemed oblivious to it all, except when he passed Fairchild. To him he gave a dignified bow.

Colonel Davis telegraphed to San Francisco: "I am happy to announce the termination of the Modoc difficulties."

He had only to make certain that, now that he had Captain Jack, he could keep him long enough to execute him. After allowing Captain Jack to change his ragged clothes, he quickly ordered that Captain Jack and Schonchin John be chained together in leg shackles. A guard of six men went to lead the men to the blacksmith. The two Modocs were told nothing. They assumed they were to be killed.

As they were being hustled past Fairchild, Captain Jack asked him where he was being taken. Fairchild reassured him saying that he should go along, and this seemed to quiet him. But when they were being shackled, both protested. A newspaperman observing the scene found himself unexpectedly moved.

> They made the most earnest protestations that they had surrendered in good faith; that they had no desire to get away, and under no circumstances should make such an attempt. It was really an affecting scene to witness the grief with which they submitted to have the shackles placed on them; but when they saw that their fate was inexorable, they made no complaint or resistance, though they felt keenly the indignity, but stood silently to let the rivets tighten to bind them in chains.

The scene of the shackling simply confirmed this correspondent's general impression of Captain Jack: "Captain Jack maintains a gloomy reserve, and will not converse with his captors on any subject. It is safe to say that he will make no explanation or revelations, but die and make no sign. Bogus Charley says all the men expect to die, and await their fate without fear. Captain Jack had no fears of what the result may be, and awaits it with stoical fortitude. He will die heroically, I have no doubt, for he has evidently less regard for life than the rest of the Modoc warriors."

Not long after Captain Jack's surrender, the Oregon volunteers reappeared on the scene. The Oregon governor had called them up again after the Second Battle for the Stronghold. Presumably, he thought they should defend Oregon settlers, if the Modocs were on the loose again. Characteristically, they took their own sweet time getting organized and making their way to the front line.

They got to the general vicinity a few days after Captain Jack's surrender. On their way they ran into group of a dozen Modocs, still at large but desperate to surrender to someone. The volunteers graciously accepted their offer, and their commander then telegraphed the

Oregon governor, "The Modoc War was ended by the Oregon Volunteers at 12 o'clock last night."

But the volunteers were not done. They first harassed a wagonload of Modoc prisoners—family groups—being transported near Lost River. Then, seven miles later, two other volunteers intercepted the wagon again, forcing the driver away at gun point. The whites executed the four men while still in the wagon (according to one account, splattering their brains all over their families).

The volunteers, of course, were untouchable patriots. The atrocity was never seriously investigated. The wagon driver, whether out of honesty or prudence, said he could identify neither of the murderers.

Back at the camp where Captain Jack and over a hundred other Modocs were under guard, Davis ordered the construction of a gallows. The Modocs had never seen one before. Scarfaced Charley asked a soldier he trusted, "What for that thing they make?"

Answer: "To hang Modocs."

Curley Headed Doctor, who had been listening, now blustered that he had medicine that "can beat that thing."

The soldier was sardonically amused: "Maybe so, Curley Headed Doctor. But, unless some other medicine interferes, you can have a chance to try it, and in the mean time, to reflect on the inhuman manner in which you and Hooker Jim killed Brotherton, Boddy, and the others."

Davis, who was still trying to decide which of the Modocs to execute summarily, brought the Boddy women to camp. They were half-hysterical facing the accused Modocs—Hooker Jim and Steamboat Frank. But the women had their own plan, and a trial was not part of it. Suddenly one pulled a pistol that she had concealed on her dress, the other a knife. They were going to kill the two Modocs right there, right then. The pistol was taken away before the woman could cock it. Davis himself grabbed the knife away, but by the blade—and he was left with a nasty cut on the heel of his hand.

Schonchin John and Captain Jack were once again led from their cells. Once again, they were worried; once again, Fairchild reassured them, "Go on. It's all right." This time they were put before what looked to be a large gun, with a large velvet cloth hanging from behind. Was Fairchild wrong this time? They were exhorted through an interpreter to remain still, not to squirm. Then the gun was uncovered, and nothing happened. And the gun was covered again. When Captain Jack and Schonchin were led away, they were smiling. They had been photographed.

8

Harper's Weekly: A Journal of Civilization (circulation 150,000) had shown no interest in the Modoc War until the assassination of Canby and Thomas. Then it treated its readers to a report almost every issue, illustrated with portraits of fallen Americans as well as panoramic illustrations of "Modocs Scalping and Torturing Prisoners" and "Soldiers Removing the Bodies of the Slain."

The editors of *Harper's* had no doubt about the lesson they thought their readers should draw from these tragic events. The Indian race was "swiftly fading around us, like the vegetation of some extinct geological era." But, in their irretrievable decline, the Indians would seek occasions to indulge "once more the untamable fury of the savage." They would, if we were not vigilant, behave "like wild beasts granted a temporary opportunity of mischief." We must therefore understand the savage mentality: "Generosity on the part of the white man is misinterpreted as timidity—a cowardly desire to buy safety, which he dare not fight for."

The same lesson that the editors of *Harper's* were drawing for their 150,000 readers was also being offered by numerous other editors in numerous periodicals throughout America. The Modoc War had left the peace policy in roughly the same shape as A. B. Meacham, not quite dead but badly scarred and headed for a long convalescence. As far as William Tecumseh Sherman was concerned, that was just fine.

Sherman had consistently and effectively used the Modoc War to advocate his military approach to the question of the western Indians. Indian-loving Christians, he thought, had truly amazing faith. Whenever their idealism became policy, the number of American graves multiplied rapidly. Praying over graves was all they were good at.

Sherman had told Canby that if the Modocs used treachery against the Peace Commission Canby should "make such use of the military force that no other Indian tribe will imitate their example, and that no other reservation for them will be necessary except graves among their chosen lava beds."

When he heard of Canby's assassination, he telegraphed Gillem urging an attack on the Modocs "so strong and persistent that their fate may be commensurate with their crime." Lest Gillem somehow miss the implication, Sherman drew it out for him: "You will be fully justified in their utter extermination."

Sherman, in the aftermath, went on the offensive against the peace advocates. To the *New York Times* he said, "Treachery is inherent in the Indian character. I know of a case where the Indians murdered the man who not two hours before had given them food and clothing." He took his offensive into the camp of the enemy. He wrote to the Quakers that since all Modocs seem to have participated in this war, all should be suitably punished—and he added, with a characteristic final sting, "if all be swept from the earth, they themselves have invited it."

Sherman was almost enjoying himself.

Gillem proved incapable of mounting the proper assault, but Davis had done the job. Sherman had only one regret about the outcome. He wrote to Phil Sheridan, "I'm sorry that Jack & most of the Modocs were not killed in the taking, for I fear they will be petted and finally turned loose . . . ready to repeat the same old Game."

To prevent this, he offered a simple solution to General Schofield, the man between Sherman and Davis in the chain of command. The leaders of the Modocs should be "tried by court martial and shot." Any others responsible for civilian casualties should be turned over to civilian authorities for trial and hanging. The rest should be "dispersed so that the name of Modoc should cease."

Davis could not have agreed more. He had decided, for the sake of military expediency, to spare the four Modoc hounds who had helped track down Captain Jack, even though he knew full well that Hooker Jim and Steamboat Frank were, as he put it, "among the worst of the Band." Indians in the future needed to know that the army would reward those who betrayed their leaders, no matter how bad their past crimes. Davis had, therefore, decided that he would summarily execute only eight to ten Modocs. The hanging was to occur at dawn on June 6th, 1873, only two days after they had arrived at his camp.

Both he and Sherman hoped that this would not give the humanitarians enough time to lobby Washington to intervene.

The attorney general himself immediately saw legal difficulties. Davis was ordered to postpone any actions until the attorney general could decide whether the Modocs were prisoners of war or simple murderers. If the latter, Davis would have to turn them over to the civilian authorities. In neither case were summary executions of the kind Davis planned approved.

Sherman was not pleased. He wired to Schofield, "I wish Davis had dispatched those Indians." However, in light of the general Indian war he expected soon to engulf the West, he thought perhaps it was wise to get the legal issues clarified now. If the Modocs were turned over to the civilian authorities, he did not doubt they would do the proper thing. The Modocs were not going to escape punishment. Sherman wrote, "I believe the same result will be accomplished in a way that will be strictly lawful, and at the same time serve as a rule for the future."

Davis did not take the broader, more patient view. Apoplectic at the unwanted interference, he talked of resigning his commission in protest: "I have no doubt of the propriety and the necessity of executing them on the spot, at once. I had no doubt of my authority as Department commander in the field to thus execute a band of outlaws, robbers and murderers like these, under the circumstances. Your dispatch indicates a long delay of the cases of the red devils, which I regret. Delays will destroy the moral effect which their prompt execution would have had upon other tribes, as also the inspiring effects upon the troops."

On June 9th the attorney general issued his decision. The Modocs had to be regarded as a nation. More particularly, they were in the peculiar legal category of a "domestic dependent nation." Since November 29th, 1872, the Modoc nation and the United States of America had been at war. He explained:

> That these hostile Indians were and are a distinct people and therefore capable of legal and legitimate war with the United States seems to me to be open to no doubt. They are in no sense citizens of the United States, and owe it no allegiance; they are governed by their own laws

and owe no obedience, and pay none, to the laws of the country in which they live; they pay nothing to the support of the Government; they occupy and possess the lands they dwell on by a quasi absolute right, and cannot be legally dispossessed of them by any power. They are dealt with only by the General Government through the instrumentality of treaties, which treaties are an evidence and acknowledgment of their independent position as distinct peoples.

That reasoning took the Modocs out of civilian jurisdiction entirely. They could be tried only by a military tribunal, and only for crimes "committed against the laws of war." They could, in short, be tried only as war criminals. Those Modocs, therefore, who should be tried were those who murderously violated the flag of truce, and those alone.

Davis, none too pleased, decided he could not remain in a temporary camp for the length of a trial. The trial would be held at Fort Klamath. He ordered a stockade to be built there out of logs, a stockade "large enough to confine 44 Bucks 49 Squaws and 62 children: total 155."

Sherman shared Davis's displeasure at the way the legal issues were resolved, and made no secret of it. He urged the secretary of war to hold the trial immediately "before some Indian agent makes a fatal promise."

Meanwhile, advocates of the peace policy mobilized behind a campaign for clemency.

Some newspapers had written extensively about the shocking murders of the Modocs who had surrendered and were in wagons, unarmed, and heading back to the reservation. Sympathetic readers wrote to the secretary of the interior asking why the white murderers were not being sought as energetically as Captain Jack and his band had been hunted down. One suggested that the only fair course was to delay the trial of the Modoc leaders until after these American murderers had been captured—and then to try the two groups simultaneously.

A correspondent from California challenged the secretary of the interior to explain to her why the Modocs were being indicted for violating the flag of truce. Did he not realize that they had learned this particular tactic from an American, Ben Wright? And that Wright, rather than being prosecuted, was treated as a hero? She asked: "Was Ben

Wright punished? No! He was rewarded with an Indian agency. A fine specimen of Indian agency was this red-handed assassin. Did our people at Yreka view Ben Wright and his brother butchers with detestation of their horrid crime? No! They turned out 'en masse' to meet the returning warriors with their bloody trophies, the Modoc scalps. They opened the Hotel to entertain the assassin guests. They sang songs and made speeches laudatory of bloody Ben Wright." If General Canby did not know all this, she added almost as an afterthought, "he was utterly unfit for the position he held."

Other advocates seized on the attorney general's opinion that the Modocs were a separate nation. If so, they reasoned, the Modoc War should be resolved not by a trial but by international arbitration.

Fairchild, Steele, and others tried to help the Modocs with a more moderate petition of their own. They did not question the government's right to try the leaders, but they did hope that the remaining Modocs would eventually be released on their own recognizance. "All of these Indians are useful farm hands, fully capable intellectually to trade for and take care of themselves." Such calm voices had little chance to be heard amidst the tumult.

Some advocates for the Modocs chose to attack Davis for his determination to execute the Modoc leaders. The American Indian Aid Association denounced this as "a ridiculous farce." Yet the association seemed less interested in the Modocs themselves than in using them as an occasion for praising Indians in general as "the only people on this continent that practice the most essential and stringent principles of Christianity." The association made this point to attack Grant's turning over Indian agencies to Christian groups: "Hence it follows that we stand more in need of missionaries from them than they need missionaries from us."

A number of congressmen also wanted to exploit the Modocs to attack Grant's policies, but on different terms. A California congressman was not satisfied with a simple trial; he wanted a full investigation. Only this "will convince the public that fraud and speculation was the cause of the war—and will I hope have some weight or influence which will go far toward convincing the government of the necessity of turning over the Indian bureau to the Military Department."

Sherman could hardly have put it better himself, although he was certain such an investigation would discover that the cause of the war was not fraud and speculation (of which there still might be plenty), but stupidity and soft-headedness. He worried, in particular, about the power of soft-headedness over his friend Grant. He knew that the Quaker-dominated Universal Peace Union had managed to get a personal audience with Grant.

The delegation from Universal Peace Union addressed President Grant "in the spirit of Him who said: 'Blessed are the peacemakers'; who taught mankind to observe the Golden Rule, and declared, 'The Son of Man is not come to destroy men's lives, but to save them'—all of which you have strongly expressed in the words: 'Let us have peace.'"

Having cited the most famous line from Grant's inaugural addresses, they as Philadelphians commended to Grant the noble example of William Penn, worthy as it was of universal imitation: "Especially was he careful that no injustice should be done to the uncultivated people who were in possession of the lands wherein he desired to found a colony by deeds of peace."

The teachings of Jesus and the example of Penn instructed us all about how the defeated Modocs should be treated.

> However false, cruel or treacherous the Indians may have been, who are now in the power of the Army of which you are the commander in chief, we ask that they may not be brutally treated and that your Peace Policy be not departed from. Among them are defenseless women and innocent children. Should their husbands, fathers and brothers be taken from them, they must of necessity suffer with them. God 'hath made of one blood all nations of men to dwell on the face of the earth.' Connected as the members of the human family are by maternal, paternal, filial and other ties, 'if one member suffer all members suffer with it.'
>
> Accepting as we trust you do these thoughts, taking them as we do to our hearts, the love of God and the love of man constrain us to plead with you and to encourage you to deal considerately and mercifully with the Indians now held by the strong arm of military law.

Ulysses S. Grant, the delegates insisted, had the opportunity through the exercise of executive clemency to "show the civilized and uncivilized worlds that there is in the soul of man a far mightier and more enduring power than any of the nations of the earth have yet brought into use." The Peace Union only hoped that "there is in many of the hearts of this great people a sufficient amount of Christian love to institute a system of measures by which these children of the forest may be educated and civilized."

Sherman, had he read the address, would have pointed out that the Indians of the West were, by and large, not children of the forest.

Nonetheless, the leaders of the Universal Peace Union could produce one woman who would scarcely be intimidated by the likes of Uncle Billy. The vice president of the group was Lucretia Coffin Mott, the same Lucretia Mott who had denounced Sherman for his contemptuous telegram on the Indian question, a telegram—she had said—that revealed Sherman as "false to humanity."

Lucretia Mott had been born on Nantucket, among the Quakers who would make that island a world center for whaling. Now past eighty and a widow, she had been a leading Quaker preacher for more than half a century.

Mott had a typical Quaker impatience with religious doctrine, declaring, "Men are judged by their likeness to Christ, rather than their notions of Christ." She also had a visionary's passion for moral causes. She had been as responsible as anyone for reviving Quaker abolitionism, the tradition of John Woolman that had lain largely dormant for a generation after his death. She had in the process argued for the connection of African emancipation and female emancipation. The right of the slave to freedom was inseparable for her from the right of women to be treated as the equals of men. These two causes she connected to the just and charitable treatment of the native races of North America.

Lucretia Mott had been a beauty—and now, although obviously suffering from the infirmities of age, she had an air of conviction about her that enabled her to mesmerize an audience. A few years before at a meeting of the Peace Union, someone questioned the connection she made between pacifism and the cause of the Indian.

Mott responded, "The treatment of the Indians may seem, by some, not to be strictly relevant to the subject of peace ... but we know in the great crime of human slavery that it never could have gone to the extent it has, but for war. So with the Indians. They never could have arrived at the state of revenge and cruelty towards the white inhabitants of this land, if they had not set the example by taking the sword."

Mott must have realized she and the others were being brushed off when they presented their memorial on behalf of the Modocs to President Grant. She was sure of it when she heard of the plans to try the Modoc leaders before a military tribunal, and she knew better than to try to get another appointment at the White House with the busy Grant.

Nonetheless, she believed, as she liked to put it, "If one is but assured of the justice of a cause, one need not hesitate to embark on the path of justice, one need not fear to go forward." President Grant might have thought he was done with Lucretia Coffin Mott on the Modoc question, but Lucretia Mott did not think she was done with him.

Mott heard that Grant was going to have dinner at the mansion of a wealthy political contributor not too far from her own residence. Mott announced that she would be going to that dinner. Her Quaker son-in-law, Edward Davis, admonished her.

"Mother, thee has no invitation, thee has not announced thy desire, etiquette demands thee to send first and see if it will be agreeable and convenient."

He should have known better.

"My spirit says go and it will not wait for etiquette. My visit is urgent! Harness the horse!"

Mott burst in upon the elegant dinner party and delivered her impassioned appeal on behalf of the accused Modocs.

Grant, after listening patiently to arguments he had heard before, tried to reason with her, explaining the pressures he was under, the nature of the crimes, the calls for revenge. Then, under her firm gaze, he wilted. He motioned to the old lady to come closer, and then had her lean toward him, and then whispered to her, "Madam, they shall not all be executed."

9

CAPTAIN JACK and the Modocs were taken, under heavy army guard, in seven large, open freight wagons back toward the Klamath reservation.

Early in the trip the warriors all stood up alert, to the considerable consternation of their guard. Then the soldiers realized what was happening. They were passing over high ground from which the Modoc men could have a last look back at the Lava Beds. They all talked briefly but rapidly among themselves in Modoc, then looked out again in silence until the Lava Beds had entirely passed from view, then huddled back down in the wagons, pulling their blankets around themselves.

The whole of the Modoc War was in that trip. From the edge of the Lava Beds to Sorass Lake, then up the east side of Tule Lake. They were now going past the little peninsula where Ben Wright massacred so many Modocs under the sign of truce. A few miles later and they were within sight of the deserted homestead of Henry Miller, the friend of the Modocs murdered in cold blood by Hooker Jim. After this cabin it was but a little ways to Bloody Point, where so many Americans had lost their lives for trespassing on Modoc land. Then around the northeast corner of Tule Lake, past the other deserted homesteads where Hooker Jim and his men had revenged themselves. Then on to Lost River where Meacham just three and a half years ago had persuaded Captain Jack to return to the reservation, and where two years ago Captain Jack and his people had returned, and where the Americans began the Modoc War little more than half a year ago by their unprovoked attack. Then up past Linkville, so long a center for agitation against the Modocs. Then the final stage to Klamath, this springtime trek in chains so unlike the winter trek three and a half years ago, when Captain Jack could insist the soldiers go ahead so that all would know he was coming in on his own. And finally the Klamath reservation, where he could see in the distance the tree under which he and David Allen had buried the hatchet for all time. And the hillside where they had all watched the new year of 1870 be born in the sky. Then on to Fort Klamath, where he had reluctantly signed the treaty in 1864 in which the Modocs gave up their rights to their traditional lands, and where he and the others were to be incarcerated, and tried, and probably killed.

Captain Jack had apparently thought hard about what he could still do for his people, now that he was defeated and a captive. He had decided that if he could implicate the Klamaths in this war, as well as Old Schonchin and the reservation Modocs, things might go easier for his own people.

As General Davis began to prepare for the trial, Captain Jack sent word that he wanted to tell him of the reservation Indians who had encouraged him in pursuing this war. After the First Battle for the Stronghold, Old Schonchin had visited Captain Jack in the Lava Beds. Old Schonchin had had a message for him from David Allen.

Captain Jack, Old Schonchin had said, should hold out, and not be fooled by the peace commissioners. "Allen said hold on to your gun. I am getting ammunition and will join you soon, have lots of people, want to get guns first. Whatever officers or commissioners saying, don't believe what they say. They are trying to fool you. They came here to fool you."

According to Captain Jack, he had been swayed by this message. "I was about to give up, was going to surrender when I got these messages. It did stir me up. When I did this thing, killed the commissioners, I expected David Allen next day or very soon."

There was much that was plausible about Captain Jack's story. Throughout the war communication was frequent between the Klamath and Yainax reservations and the Modocs holed up in the Lava Beds. The Indians knew the land too well for the army to cut off Captain Jack and his people completely.

Moreover, the Klamath scouts had done very badly in the First Battle for the Stronghold, worse even than the Oregon volunteers. Opinion was mixed about whether this poor performance was due to cowardice or treachery. But no one doubted that the Klamaths had proven worthless in fighting against Modocs. That was why the Warm Springs scouts had been brought in.

Captain Jack knew he could play on the Americans' greatest fear, that of a general Indian uprising. Whenever the Modocs had a success, rumors had swirled through Oregon, California, and northern Nevada about other Indian groups about to join the Modocs on the war path.

After the Battle of Lost River, Odeneal had warned that if the Modocs were not quickly defeated "a guerrilla warfare would be waged until every settler in that region would be murdered; and other Indians, now peaceable, seeing their success would hasten to join them, and the result would be the most gigantic Indian war of modern times."

Newspapers had taken up the cry. By the next spring the *Portland Daily Bulletin* treated it as common knowledge that "if the soldiers did not whip Jack all Indians would join in a general war of extermination."

Davis himself had been informed by his headquarters that this Modoc War threatened to spread. From across the whole Western frontier came numerous reports "of unusual movement and insolence among the various Indian tribes."

Captain Jack had to know he was making charges Davis would not be able to ignore.

Davis did not ignore them. He investigated them energetically. This meant that Captain Jack had to confront once again the formidable David Allen. Allen was called before Davis and responded to Captain Jack's allegations with his characteristic aplomb:

> I never advised any Indians to go on the war path. No white man or Indian ever heard me say anything of that kind. I made a speech to Meacham four years ago and said I didn't want to make war; that I never had nor would fight against the whites; and what I said then I stand by now.
>
> I have always studied to live in peace with the white men. I always want to be able to face those men who have always known me. I am glad to face the soldier tyee so that he can judge if I tell the truth.
>
> Everything went right enough until lately. There are men who give

false reports of what I say. Now General Davis will get to hear from my mouth and from no one else's.

David Allen recounted briefly his various negotiations with white *tyees* before the war, during the war, and after the war. Then he contrasted his behavior with Captain Jack's. "I have studied and wondered for a long time why Captain Jack did not come here to live. I advised him to come, and his Modoc relatives at Yainax advised him to come. He always turned a deaf ear and would not listen.

"Now I want to know why Captain Jack accused me on account of things he has done himself. I was sure, all the while, that he would have to come or that the soldiers would finally bring him. Captain Jack now sees that I told him the truth. I feel that I did my duty towards him in advising him to come here as I did."

A suspicious Davis tried to challenge Allen through interrogation. How did he explain his people's behavior during the war?

"When the war broke out, I was sick. My heart was good towards the whites."

Answer the question. Didn't some of his people support the Modocs in the war?

"All I know is that a number of my people went down to the lava beds to help fight Captain Jack."

Didn't they on occasion supply him with ammunition?

"I don't know one that gave them any. If I did, I would tell of it."

Didn't he send a message to Captain Jack through Old Schonchin?

"I didn't know Schonchin was going there when he went."

Old Schonchin himself was then brought in, and he denied ever having taken a message to Captain Jack.

Now the Modoc was brought in, and he seemed cowed by David Allen. Under close examination he admitted that he had not been told Allen's message personally by Schonchin. He had heard about it from others, from Steamboat Frank and Bogus Charley and Boston Charley.

David Allen interrupted him, saying that he always found that stories changed remarkably as they traveled from one person to another.

Captain Jack, now visibly unnerved, could only repeat his allegations against David Allen, and assure Davis he could point out all who

had urged him to continue fighting once Davis had his leg irons removed.

Davis ended the inquiry without bothering to reply.

The trial of Captain Jack, Schonchin John, Black Jim, Boston Charley,
and the two boys, Slolux and Barncho, is held in the hall of Klamath
Fort. The military tribunal arrays itself along a narrow table. Tobey
and Frank Riddle are there as interpreters. The four Modoc men sit on
a bench, while the two boys lounge on the floor, apparently oblivious to
what is happening, sometimes even asleep. A file of soldiers—the
guard—stands at alert, their rifles with bayonets. At the back of the
crowd of spectators, many of them newspapermen, stand Hooker Jim,
Bogus Charley, Shacknasty Jim, and Steamboat Frank, whose late service to the army has rendered them immune from prosecution. The
business of the trial begins on July 5, 1873, promptly at 10 A.M.

Charge first: "Murder in violation of the laws of war." This was
specifically in regards to the deaths of General E. R. S. Canby and Reverend Eleasar Thomas.

Charge second: "Assault with intent to kill in violation of the laws of
war." This was specifically in regards to the attempts to kill peace commissioners A. B. Meacham and L. S. Dyar.

"All this at or near the Lava Beds, so-called, situated near Tule
Lake, in the State of California, on or about the 11th day of April, 1873."

How do the accused plead? Each one, through an interpreter, pleads
not guilty to both charges.

The first witness is the interpreter, Frank Riddle. He identifies
each of the Modocs and places them at the assassination. He also in-
structs the court about the relative importance of each defendant in
the tribal hierarchy. Captain Jack is "a chief amongst them." Schonchin
is a "sub-chief," the American army equivalent being a "sergeant."
Black Jim was just a sentry; Boston Charley only a "high private." The
boys Barncho and Slolux, "not anything."

Riddle then recounts at length the various warnings he and Tobey
received that treachery was planned against the commissioners, how
he had tried to dissuade Canby and the commissioners from walking

into the trap, and how he had been ignored. Then he tells what happened at the meeting—the cigars, the various speeches, then Captain
Jack shooting Canby under the eye and the bullet coming out the back
of his head.

"I jumped and ran then, and never stopped to look back any more. I
saw General Canby fall over, and I expected he was killed, and I
jumped and ran with all my might. I never looked back but once, and
when I looked back Mr. Meacham was down, and my woman was down,
and there was an Indian standing over Mr. Meacham. Mr. Meacham
was sort of lying down this way [showing how], and had one of his
hands sticking out."

The judge, not satisfied, asks, "As soon as Captain Jack fired, what
then occurred?"

"They commenced firing all around. I could not tell who was firing
except Schonchin here. I see him firing at Mr. Meacham, but the others
were kind of up in behind me, and they were firing, and I did not turn
around to look to see who it was. I thought it was warm times there."

The amusement which this last comment prompts from the gallery
doesn't please the court, although Riddle himself is clearly pleased
with it.

Tobey Riddle and L. S. Dyar then confirm parts of Frank Riddle's
testimony. After that, the court adjourns until Monday, July 7th.

This day is devoted to the testimony of Shacknasty Jim, Steamboat
Frank, Bogus Charley, and Hooker Jim. They eagerly confirm the role
of the defendants, and incidentally their own roles, in planning and carrying out the assassination. A high point of sorts is reached when
Hooker Jim is asked, "Are you now a friend to Captain Jack?" and answers, "I have been a friend of Captain Jack, but I don't know what he
got mad at me for."

Near the end of this testimony, there is a stir in the courtroom.
A. B. Meacham has arrived, and all eyes are on him, studying him for
signs of his maiming, some of which are easy to see. He obviously has
no use of his right hand at all, and a finger on his left is mangled. A
large scar crosses his forehead—and an ugly lump shows where the
bullet entered near his eye. He moves slowly, carefully, like an old man.

The prisoners themselves seem stunned to see him, as if they had
not believed he had survived his wounds, although they had been told.

Meacham has tried to follow the course of events since he returned to Salem. He is appalled at Davis's decision to give amnesty to the four Modoc hounds. Even if they had been promised this by those in authority, the decision is still, he thinks, "unjust." Captain Jack's attempt to implicate the Klamaths only saddens Meacham: "Nothing new . . . has been brought out implicating outside parties in either the matter of assassination or of the origin of the war." Nonetheless, Meacham is here this day to try to do his part.

Just before adjournment, he is briefly interrogated by the court, but he has little to add to what has already been said. Nonetheless, Meacham is visibly disturbed. He wants to point out the extenuating circumstances, but is not asked the right questions. After adjournment he seeks out Colonel Elliot, who is the judge in the trial.

"Have the prisoners no counsel?"

"They have been unable to obtain counsel. The usual question was asked them."

"It seems to me that, for the honor and credit of the Government, and in order to have all the facts drawn out and placed on record, counsel should have been appointed."

"We are perfectly willing, and would much prefer it; but there is no lawyer here, and we must go on without."

Meacham is becoming increasingly indignant, although his doctors have told him he should spare himself excitement.

"I have no disposition to shield the prisoners from justice, but I do feel that to close up all gaps, and make the record complete, all the circumstances should be drawn out. Not because anything could be shown to justify their crimes, but because it is in harmony with right and justice. Sooner than have it said that this was an ex-parte trial, I will appear myself as their counsel, by your consent."

Elliot is now trying not to sound weary in the face of sanctimony, and he most emphatically does not want trouble.

"Certainly, we are willing, and if you say you will appear as their counsel, we will have your name entered on the record. Certainly, Mr. Meacham, we are more than willing."

Meacham has allowed himself to get carried away. He does not feel able to defend the Modocs. Physically perhaps he is up to it, but psychologically he is filled with revulsion.

Nonetheless, he hurries over to the guardhouse, to consult with his prospective clients. When the men are brought in, Meacham involuntarily shudders at the sound of their chains, which are of brightly polished steel and sparkle as if jeweled whenever hit by the sunlight through the barred windows.

The Modocs are obviously happy to see Old Man Meacham, and extend their hands. But he refuses to shake, addressing himself to Captain Jack.

"No, Captain Jack, your hands are red with Canby's blood. I cannot, now."

Captain Jack withdraws his hand, but Schonchin keeps his out. So Meacham turns to address him.

"No, Schonchin, your hands are red with my own blood. I cannot, I will not now."

Schonchin, not deterred, reaches out further and squeezes Meacham's arm, with a grunt of satisfaction. For a moment Meacham is perplexed, and then thinks that perhaps this is a test to see if he really is flesh and blood or just a ghost come back from the spirit realm to haunt them. But this is not the line of inquiry Meacham wants to pursue.

"Why did you not have a lawyer to talk for you?"

Captain Jack seems eager to answer.

"I don't know any lawyer that understands this affair. They do not do me any good. Everybody is against me. Even the Modocs are turned against me. I have but few friends. I am alone."

So Elliot was telling the truth, but Captain Jack should not allow his despair to deprive him of a fair trial. The Modoc looks decades older than the last time Meacham saw him. The confidence, the dignity, the sense of purpose, even the appearance of physical strength, all are gone. He seems to be suffering a kind of general palsy; his hands, his whole body is slightly trembling constantly, like an aspen in a breeze.

Meacham cannot let his mind wander; he has to keep it focused on the business at hand.

"You can talk yourself. The newspapers say, 'Captain Jack has spoken for his race; now let extermination be the cry.'"

"I know that the white man has many voices. They tell one side, they do not tell the other."

"Tell the other yourself. You can talk. Now speak for your race. Tell the other side. The world will read it."

Captain Jack is staring at him now. After a brief pause, he says emphatically, "Meacham, you talk for me."

Meacham now knows that this is impossible. He realized it when he could not bring himself to shake Captain Jack's hand.

"No, Captain Jack, I cannot talk for you. I saw you kill General Canby. I cannot talk for you. If you had shot me as Schonchin did, I would talk for you. As it is, I cannot."

His reasoning seems to lead to the conclusion that he can defend Schonchin, who immediately begins to brighten. This in turn disgusts Meacham, who has never respected him.

Meacham says emphatically, "I will not talk for Schonchin. He was all the time in favor of blood."

Schonchin looks hurt and tries to cajole Meacham.

"I did not kill you. You did not die. I am an old man. I was excited. I did not shoot good. The others all laughed at me. I quit. You shoot me. You don't want me to die. You did not die."

Captain Jack is in no mood for such banter, any more than Meacham is. The Modoc wants Meacham to realize that he will not be able to speak for himself.

He pleads, "I cannot talk with the chains on my legs. My heart is not strong, when the chain is on my leg. You can talk strong. You talk for me."

Meacham is wavering in his resolve as he leaves. Captain Jack, whom he so respected, still respects as the best of the Modocs, is now pitiful, almost whining. He is right. He will not be able to talk effectively for himself.

Within an hour Meacham has convened some friends to discuss the possibility of his entering the trial as counsel for the defense. They are of one voice in rejecting this. Meacham is not sufficiently recovered from his wounds. If the trial does not kill him, the storm of protest that would engulf him in its aftermath will. He is just too weak.

They tell him what he hopes to hear. They quiet, or at least temporarily drown out, his conscience. He will not defend Captain Jack.

On July 8th the defense has its opportunity to present witnesses. Captain Jack, who is representing himself, calls Scarfaced Charley. He corroborates at length Captain Jack's discredited story that the Klamaths had encouraged the Modocs to resist the army. Neither Charley nor Captain Jack seems to realize that this, even if true, is irrelevant to the charges. Captain Jack calls two minor Modocs to confirm Charley's testimony, and then says he has no further testimony to offer.

The court informs him that he has the right to make a statement. He complains that he cannot talk very well with irons on his legs. He then gives a long rambling statement, full of excuses and empty of arguments.

Meacham is embarrassed for him. In his memoirs he writes, "It is evident that he feels the hopelessness of his cause; that he is no longer the brave, strong man that he was when free and untrammeled. . . . He is now unmanned, and the chief who has made so great a name as a warrior is now a mere pettifogger."

Captain Jack tries to shift responsibility from himself to the war party in his band, those very four who have been given amnesty. At a certain point he suddenly pauses, realizes the whole speech is a mistake, says apologetically that he cannot talk very well with leg irons, and abruptly sits down.

Schonchin Jim then jumps up, excitedly repeats the charges of Scarfaced Charley against the Klamaths, then sits down. None of the other defendants wish to speak.

The court does not take long in reaching a verdict. All are guilty on all counts; they are all sentenced to be hung by the neck until death. The date for the executions is set at October 3rd, 1873.

The court formally pardons the Modocs who turned army scout. The judge explains, "I believe that there could be no better policy than that of teaching these savages that treachery to their race, under such circumstances as those which obtained here, would merit its own sure reward."

The Modocs, it is known, have a special dread of death by hanging. They believe that such a death will trap the soul within their body forever. Those killed in this way will never be free of this life.

Captain Jack tries to talk about this to Meacham when he visits him after the trial, but Meacham does not listen. He just wants to assure Captain Jack that the trial was fair, the sentence just. Captain Jack complains that only one side of the story was told and that he had no friends to talk for him. Meacham understands the implied accusation against himself. He promises that when he fully recovers from his wounds he will write out a fair statement of what happened that all can read. Captain Jack grasps his hand as if not wanting him to leave. Meacham pulls himself away, distraught. He will not speak with him again. He hurries away from Klamath, back to his family.

On an open meadow at the fort a long scaffold is erected with six ropes. It is noted that this is a much more finished piece of work than the one Davis had wanted to use at Tule Lake. The traitor Modoc scouts, with free run of the fort, take particular interest in this scaffold and are full of questions for its builders about how it works. They seem overjoyed at their good fortune.

Scarfaced Charley also has the run of the fort. He refuses to associate with the Modoc scouts. He is also unable to bring himself to visit Captain Jack or the others. He is usually seen sitting alone, doing nothing.

The day before the execution an official delegation visits Captain Jack, including the colonel now in charge of the fort, Frank Wheaton, and the post chaplain, Father Charles Hegemborg. Hegemborg explains that Christ died for all men; if they accept Him, they can still be saved. Captain Jack and Schonchin, in particular, seem attentive. They are very worried about their souls being trapped in their bodies.

Wheaton then explains to them that the president has rejected the appeal to have their sentences commuted. After Wheaton finishes, there is a deathly silence.

Captain Jack is now speaking to Wheaton, but so softly he can barely be understood.

"I have heard the sentence, and I know what it means. When I look in my heart, I see no crime. I was in favor of peace. The young men were not ready for peace. They carried me with them. I feel that while these four men—Bogus, Shacknasty, Hooker, and Steamboat—are free, they have triumphed over me and over the government. When I surrendered, I expected to be pardoned, and to live with my people on Klamath land."

Wheaton asks Jack which Modoc he wishes to take over for him after his death. Jack answers only indirectly.

"I can think of no one. I cannot trust even Scarfaced Charley."

Wheaton makes a mental note to appoint Scarfaced Charley as Captain Jack's successor. Wheaton then encourages Captain Jack to think about what the chaplain has said.

Captain Jack responds, "I know that what he says is good, and I shall follow his advice."

Wheaton and Hegemborg are momentarily encouraged by this.

Then Captain Jack adds absently, "I should like to live until I die a natural death."

Slolux and Barncho then begin to behave like the boys they are. They plead that they had no part in the assassination. For the first time they seem to realize that they are scheduled to die. They swear they did not do it, and promise never to do it again.

Black Jim tries another tack. If he is permitted to live, he could take care of his tribe, become Captain Jack's successor. This is met with an awkward pause.

Then Black Jim says hopefully, "I don't know what Captain Jack and Schonchin think of it."

Captain Jack just shakes his head.

Seeing this, Black Jim becomes defiant: "If the white chief's law says I am guilty of crime, let me die. I am not afraid to die. I am afraid of nothing."

Then he turns to the priest: "I should like to hear the spirit man's talk."

Ignoring him, Captain Jack now requests that the execution be delayed so the president can read his words. Perhaps the president does not know that Captain Jack did not want the murders.

Now it is Wheaton's turn to shake his head.

At this, Boston Charley, who has gradually become more and more agitated during the whole interview, erupts:

You all know me. During the war it seemed to me that I had two hearts—one Indian and the other white. I am only a boy, and yet I know what I have done. Although a boy, I feel like a man, and when I look on each side of me I think of these other men as women. I do not fear death. I think I am the only man in the room. I fought in the front rank with Shacknasty, Steamboat, Bogus, and Hooker. I am altogether a man, and not half a woman. I killed Dr. Thomas. Steamboat and Bogus helped. Bogus said to me, "Do you believe that these commissioners mean to try to make peace?" I said, "I believe so." He said, "I don't. They want to lead us into some trap." I said, "All right. I go with you." I would like to see all my people and bid them good-by today. I would like to go to the stockade to see them. I see that if I were to blame others it would not amount to anything. I see it is too late. I know that other chief men were not at the bottom of that affair, and they did not take so big a part in the massacre as the younger men. I know but little, but when I see anything with my eyes, I know it.

Captain Jack, trying to act as if this outburst had not happened, insists that at least Hooker and Bogus be tried for their part.

When nobody so much as responds, he then says with finality, "If I am to die, I am ready to go to see my great Father in the spirit world."

Schonchin, competitive as always, will not allow Captain Jack to have the last word. He expands on this religious theme:

The Great Spirit, who looks from above, will see Schonchin in chains, but He knows that this heart is good, and says, "You die, you become one of my people." I will not try to believe that the President is doing according to the will of the Great Spirit in condemning me to die. You may all look at me and see that I am firm and resolute. I am trying to think that it is just that I should die, and that the Great Spirit approves of this and says it is law. I am to die. I leave my son. I hope he will be allowed to remain in this country. I hope he will grow up like a good man. I want to turn him over to the old chief Schonchin at Yainax, who will make a good man of him.

Thoughts of his son Peter lead Schonchin to think of the other young men, those who insisted on killing the peace commissioners, and this leads him to review once again the circumstances of the war and the killings, especially those that mitigated his own guilt. But then he catches himself. He is not going to make excuses or plead. The time for that has passed.

"You are the law-giving parties. You say I must die. I am satisfied, if the law is correct."

Now he is obviously looking to conclude, searching for the right words:

"I have made a straight speech. I would like to see the Big Chief face to face and talk with him. But he is a long distance off, like at the top of a high hill with me at the bottom, and I cannot go to him. But he has made his decision—and I say, let me die. I do not talk to cross the decision. My heart tells me I should not die, that you do me a great wrong in taking my life. War is a terrible thing. All must suffer, the best horses, the best cattle and the best men. I can now only say, Let Schonchin die."

He is done. Neither Captain Jack nor Charley nor Black Jim nor the boys show any inclination to speak again. So the chaplain says a closing prayer. Then he and Wheaton leave.

The next morning, October 3rd, 1873, Father Hegemborg, in saying a last prayer over the condemned Modocs in their cell, breaks down. While his words are being translated into Modoc, he puts his head in his hands and begins to weep. Wheaton, wanting this over, assures the Modocs he will respect their wishes regarding their remains.

The six condemned Modocs are transported to the scaffold by wagon. When they reach it, the two boys are told to stay behind, their first indication that they are to be spared. Grant has kept his promise to Lucretia Mott.

A large crowd gathers, a few thousand. Soldiers, settlers, newspapermen. The Modoc hounds are there. Scarfaced Charley is not.

According to one account, when the four condemned Modocs are on the scaffold with the ropes about to be fitted around their necks, a settler in the crowd yells out, "Jack! What would you give me to take your place?"

Jack seeks out the heckler, and then says firmly, "Five hundred ponies and both my wives."

These are his last recorded words.

Epilogue

SHORTLY AFTER the executions, the Modoc captives were transported to Oklahoma, where they supported themselves on 180 acres of wheat and corn. Slolux joined them there in 1878, having served five years of a life sentence in the military prison at Alcatraz Island. Barncho died on Alcatraz while still in captivity.

Scarfaced Charley was named chief, but he did not last long. He refused to cooperate with officials in Oklahoma, who wanted him to suppress traditional Modoc gambling games. He was replaced by the more accommodating Bogus Charley. In the 1880s Scarfaced Charley was converted by a Quaker missionary.

Fort Klamath, the fort that had always been in the wrong place, was abandoned as no longer needed in 1890. That was the same year the Sioux danced the Ghost Dance, left their reservation, and were slaughtered at Wounded Knee, the last battle of the Western Indian wars, the final closing of the frontier.

A little later Gillem's Graveyard would be dug up, and the remains found transported East to be reinterred at Arlington National Cemetery with full military honors.

In 1909 the Modocs were permitted to return to live on the Yainax reservation. Thereabouts many of their descendants still reside today. A few remained in Oklahoma. Despite William Tecumseh Sherman's wish to the contrary, the Modocs endured as a people.

A. B. Meacham fulfilled his promise to Captain Jack to record the facts of the Modoc War as he knew them. His *Wigwam and War-path* was published in 1875. For a few years he then traveled across America, lecturing on his experiences. He was usually accompanied by Frank and Tobey Riddle, Scarfaced Charley, and other Modocs to give his talks a sense of authenticity. A. B. Meacham died at his desk in 1882, having become arguably the foremost advocate of Indian rights of his generation.

The hard life of the camp did not do well by the American commanders. Gillem never shook the illness that incapacitated him during the war. He died a few years later at the age of forty-five. Davis did not long survive him, dying at the age of fifty-one. Wheaton did better. He retired from the army in the 1890s, just in time to miss the Spanish American War.

John Fairchild was still ranching near Hot Creek in the early twentieth century. By then Peter Schonchin, Schonchin John's son, who had maimed his hand taking booty after the First Battle for the Stronghold, had become another respected rancher of the border country of Oregon and California.

Tule Lake is now a recreation area, its size much diminished because Lost River has been diverted from it. During the Second World War the shore of Tule Lake was the site of an internment camp for Japanese-Americans.

The Lava Beds themselves were made a National Monument in 1925 and are run today by the National Park Service. To approach the region by road from the east, you must pass through a county named Modoc and a small town named Canby.

Sources

Two works have proven essential to the writing of this narrative:

Hagen, Olaf (ed.). *The Modoc War Correspondence.* Unpublished manuscript, Bancroft Library, University of California at Berkeley, 1942, a 2,000-page compilation of manuscripts concerning the war.

Meacham, Alfred B. *Wigwam and War-path.* Boston: Dale, 1875. An extensive memoir by a central figure.

Two secondary works have proven invaluable:

Murray, Keith. *The Modocs and Their War.* Norman: University of Oklahoma Press, 1959.

Thompson, Erwin. *Modoc War: Its Military History and Topography.* Sacramento: Argus, 1971.

Both of these are careful, scholarly attempts to reconstruct the events of the war with a minimum of interpretation; the latter is much enhanced by the maps of Harry Scott.

Of the many other sources consulted, the following have been useful:

Applegate, Lindsay. "Notes and Reminiscences." *Oregon Historical Society Quarterly* 22 (1922): 12–45. On the establishment of the Applegate Trail.

Athearn, Robert. *William Tecumseh Sherman and the Settlement of the West.* Norman: University of Oklahoma Press, 1956. An able presentation of Uncle Billy's point of view.

Belich, James. *The New Zealand Wars.* London: Penguin, 1986. *I Shall Not Die.* Wellington, 1989. Two works important for comparative purposes.

Bland, T. A. *Life of Albert Meacham.* Washington: Bland, 1983. A brief panegyric.

Boyle, William Henry. *Personal Observations on the Conduct of the Modoc War.* Los Angeles: Dawson, 1959. Richard Dillon's edition of an important memoir.

Brady, Cyrus. *Northwestern Fights and Fighters*. New York: Doubleday, 1909. Contains a number of memoirs, including Boutelle's and Ivan Applegate's.

Brown, Wilfrid. *This Was a Man*. North Hollywood: privately printed, 1971. On Jesse Applegate.

Brown, William. *California Northeast: The Bloody Ground*. Oakland: Biobooks, 1954. Primarily of interest for Hardin's recollections.

Cromwell, Otelia. *Lucretia Mott*. Cambridge: Harvard University Press, 1958. A fine biography of a woman who deserves even better.

Curtin, Jeremiah. *Myths of the Modocs*. Boston: Little, Brown, 1912. Wonderful myths blandly recounted.

Dillon, Richard. *Burnt Out Fires*. Englewood Cliffs: Prentice Hall, 1973. An accurate if breezily written narrative of the war.

DuBois, Cora. "The 1870 Ghost Dance." *University of California Anthropological Records* 3 (1939): 1–151. The most complete account.

Elia, Donald. "The Argument over Civilian or Military Indian Control, 1965–80." *Historian* 24 (1961-62): 207–25.

Fitzgerald, Maurice. "The Modoc War: Reminiscences." *Americana* 21 (1927): 498–521.

Fradkin, Philip. *The Seven States of California*. New York: Holt, 1995. Chapter 3: An engaging journalistic evocation of the region.

Fritz, Henry. *The Movement for Indian Assimilation, 1860–90*. Philadelphia, 1963. Still important because it emphasizes the sectarianism of the peace policy.

Greene, Dana (ed.). *Lucretia Mott: Her Complete Speeches and Sermons*. New York, 1980.

Heymann, Marc. *Prudent Soldier*. Glendale, 1959. A competent biography of Canby.

Kaliher, Michael. "The Applegate Trail, 1846 to 1853." *Journal of the Shaw Historical Library* 1 (1986): 6–23.

Keller, Robert. *American Protestantism and United States Indian Policy, 1869–82*. Lincoln: University of Nebraska Press, 1983. A careful monograph on Sherman's opponents that still needs to be supplemented by Fritz.

Knight, Oliver. *Following the Indian Wars*. Norman: University of Oklahoma Press, 1960. An adequate survey of press coverage.

Landrum, Francis. *Guardhouse, Gallows, and Graves*. Klamath Falls, 1988. A very convenient compilation of sources on the trial and execution.

Meacham, A. B., *Winema*. Hartford: American, 1876. An unconvincing attempt to present Tobey Riddle as a nineteenth-century Pocahontas.

Mooney, James. *The Ghost Dance Religion and the Sioux Outbreak of 1890*. Washington, D.C.: Smithsonian, 1896. The classic account of the Ghost Dance, although centered on a later episode.

Muir, John. *Steep Trails*. Boston: Little, Brown, 1918. Containing a brief, but suggestive evocation of Modoc country.

Nash, Phileo. "The Place of Religious Revivalism in the Formation of the Intercultural Community on Klamath Reservation." *Social Anthropology of North American Tribes*, (Frank Eggan, ed.). Chicago: University of Chicago Press, 1955. Dreadfully written but useful.

Odeneal, T. B. *The Modoc War*. Portland: Portland Bulletin, 1873. A self-serving account of its origin.

Parke, John. "A Visit to the Lava Beds." *Journal of the United States Infantry Association* 4 (1908): 710–38. Accompanied at first by Fairchild.

Putnam, Charles. "Incidents of the Modoc War." *Journal of the Shaw Historical Library* 1 (1987): 1–12. An interesting memoir.

Ray, Verne. *Primitive Pragmatists*. Seattle: University of Washington Press, 1963. The best general treatment of the traditional Modoc way of life.

Reed, Gregory. *An Historical Geography Analysis of the Modoc War*. Chico, 1991. A game effort that adds a little to Thompson's topographical approach.

Rickey, Don. *Forty Miles a Day on Beans and Hay*. Norman: University of Oklahoma Press, 1963. An engaging sketch of army life on the frontier for the rank and file.

Riddle, Jeff. *The Indian History of the Modoc War*. San Francisco: Moses, 1914. An attempt to present the Modocs' side, which unintentionally demeans them in the process.

Seymour, Flora. *Indian Agents on the Old Frontier*. New York: Appleton Century, 1914. With a chapter on Meacham that effectively places him and his agency in a broader context.

Simpson, William. *Meeting the Sun*. London: Longmans, 1874. An English adventurer on a round-the-world trip happens upon the Modoc War (and is shocked by the swearing in Yreka).

Stern, Theodore. *The Klamath Tribe*. Seattle: University of Washington Press, 1965. A general historical treatment with much about the Modocs.

Thompson, William. *Reminiscences of a Pioneer*. San Francisco, 1912. The war as remembered by a proud Oregon volunteer.

Thornton, Russell. *We Shall Live Again*. Cambridge, England: Cambridge University Press, 1986. A sociological analysis of nativist revival movements.

Utley, Robert. *Frontier Regulars*. New York, 1974; *The Indian Frontier of the American West*. Albuquerque: University of New Mexico Press, 1984. Two able overviews.

Waltmann, Henry. "Circumstantial Reformer." *Arizona and the West* 13 (1970): 323–42. A persuasive, revisionist account of Grant's Indian policy.

Wells, Harry. *The West Shore* 10 (1884). Three articles on the early history of the Modocs, including the Ben Wright massacre.

Newspaper articles from the *New York Herald, San Francisco Chronicle, San Francisco Evening Bulletin, Yreka Journal,* and *Yreka Union* have been consulted—but have contributed surprisingly little. Also consulted were surviving issues of Thomas's *The California Christian Advocate* (most of the 1872 issues did not survive) and the anonymous articles on the Modoc War published in *Harper's Weekly: A Journal of Civilization* between April 26 and June 28, 1873.